COLDWATER AQUARIUMS

Coldwater Aquariums

AND SIMPLE OUTDOOR POOLS

---

by Neil Wainwright

With line illustrations in the text by
BAZ EAST
and four pages of black and white
photographs

FREDERICK WARNE & CO LTD
FREDERICK WARNE & CO INC
London · New York

© Frederick Warne & Co Ltd
London, England
1969
Reprinted 1970
Reprinted 1972
Reprinted 1976

ISBN 0 7232 1086 1

ACKNOWLEDGMENTS

The author and publishers wish to thank Mr. John Clegg
for permission to reproduce photographs on plates 1, 3
(top left and below) and 4, and Messrs. Highlands Water
Gardens for plates 2 and 3 (top right).

Library of Congress Catalog
Card No 69-20108

Printed in Great Britain by
W & J Mackay Limited, Chatham
782.1175

Contents

List of Plates

I

Your Goldfish

Have you ever kept a goldfish?

If so, you were probably disappointed and felt that fish-keeping was not a particularly interesting hobby. The fish just swam round and round in its bowl, keeping as close as it could to the top of it, and ignoring the ants' eggs and bread that you gave it. The goldfish bowl looked quite nice standing on a window ledge with the sun shining through it, but after a time even that was spoiled by the bright green weed-like plant that grew on the inside of the bowl. It is perfectly possible that you won the fish and its bowl at a fair-ground, so it did not cost you much money, but it was rather annoying that it should die after you had had it for only a short time.

Such an experience is quite common and the trouble is nothing to do with the goldfish as such. The fish described above had been kept under the worst possible conditions and it is hardly surprising that it failed to live. The really surprising thing is that so many goldfish survive under conditions that are almost as bad, which goes to prove that it is really a hardy little fish.

Kept under proper conditions the goldfish can be an interesting creature to study. It may be kept indoors in a tank or outdoors in a pool, and, as we shall see later, a pool can be made at practically no cost. The upkeep of the fish costs only a few pence each week, and starting the hobby is not an expensive business.

The goldfish is what is known as a 'coldwater' breed, that is to say its tank does not need artificial heating. There are many other coldwater breeds that may be kept in the same way as goldfish, and more will be said about these later. As most people start the hobby of fish-keeping with goldfish, however, it is this breed that will first be considered.

If we are to make a good job of keeping goldfish we must first know how a fish breathes and lives, and what it needs in its surroundings if it is to thrive.

The most noticeable parts of a fish are its fins. In some ways each fin may be thought of as a fan, because it has a number of 'spines' (resembling the sticks of a fan) connected by thin tissue. Some fish have small 'adipose fins' and these carry no spines, but in the case of all fins that have the spines the fish can raise or lower the fin in almost the same way as a fan is opened and shut.

Fig. 1 shows the outline of a fish with the arrangement of the fins. This drawing is not intended to represent any particular breed of fish, but is simply a general guide so that you will be able to identify

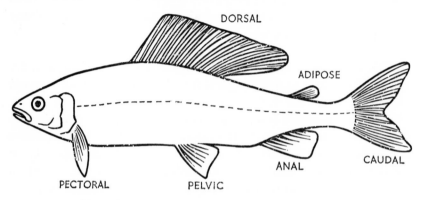

Fig. 1 Outline of a fish showing arrangement of fins

and name the fins correctly. This may be of importance if you take to fish-keeping seriously, and read more advanced books than this about the hobby.

At the back of the body is what is usually called the tail, though its correct title is 'caudal fin'. There is a large fin (the 'dorsal') along the middle line of the top of the fish, and with some breeds there is a small 'adipose' fin set behind this. Towards the front of the fish but on the underside of it there are two small 'pectoral' fins, one on each side of the body. Behind these are the larger 'pelvic' fins (again, one on each side of the body) while the large, single 'anal' fin is situated between the pelvic and caudal fins. You will have no trouble in identifying these fins from fig. 1.

According to the breed of fish these fins may be of different size or shape, but this does not affect the job that they have to do. The pectoral fins help the fish to steer, or to slow itself down, the caudal fin assists in driving the fish forward (more especially when it needs to make a sudden spurt), while the job of the remaining fins is to keep the body of the fish in the proper upright position, or, as a sailor would say, 'on an even keel'.

Although we do not think of a fish 'breathing' in the way that we usually mean the word, oxygen is as essential to fish as it is to human beings. The only oxygen that they can get comfortably, however, is dissolved in water, so they have 'gills' by which they can pass the oxygen into their blood.

What happens is this.

The fish takes in a mouthful of water and passes it through its gill openings. These openings are hidden under the 'gill-covers' which are always noticeable in a fish (they are the bony plates on each side of the head). The gills extract the oxygen from the water and pass it into the blood-stream, and the unwanted water is then passed out behind the gill-plates.

You might think that if a fish lived in a small tank it would, sooner or later, take all the oxygen out of the water and then die for lack of it.

There are two things that prevent this.

Firstly, in a well-kept aquarium tank certain underwater plants are rooted, and these plants manufacture a small but useful amount of oxygen which they release into the water. Much more important than this is the fact that water in contact with air absorbs oxygen from it. The larger the area of water in such contact the more oxygen that can be absorbed, and the more fish that can be kept under conditions that are really satisfactory for them.

As well as taking in oxygen the fish 'breathes' out carbon dioxide, which finds its way to the top of the water where it is dispersed into the air. The more carbon dioxide there is in the water the less room there is for the life-giving oxygen.

Perhaps you are now beginning to suspect one of the reasons why your goldfish did not thrive in its small bowl.

3

In case you are still not sure, take a look at fig. 2. This represents an ordinary goldfish bowl of the kind you are often offered in pet shops. When you pour water into such a bowl the surface of the water will, of course, be of a circular shape. You will see that two

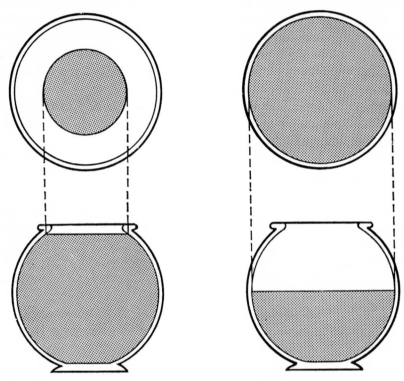

Fig. 2 Surface area of water in goldfish bowls

lines have been drawn across the bowl, one halfway up and the other towards the top of it. If you fill the bowl to the top line (as most people do) you will have a water area similar to the circle shown on the left. When the bowl is only half-filled you have the much larger water area shown on the right.

In other words, the half-filled bowl is giving more oxygen to the fish than is the filled bowl.

4

Any fish unlucky enough to be kept in a small filled bowl soon finds itself short of oxygen. It then moves to the top of the water where it tries to gulp oxygen direct from the air, but having got there it has very little room in which to move round. This is as near cruelty to the fish as makes no difference.

Apart from anything else the shape of the ordinary goldfish bowl is wasteful of space. Fig. 3, A represents a goldfish bowl (as seen from above) standing in a rectangular shaping that just touches the extreme edges of the bowl. The shaded patches outside the circle

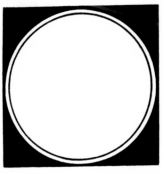

A

B

Fig. 3 *A* Goldfish bowl, seen from above, shown in a rectangular shape

B Side-view of goldfish bowl, shown in a rectangular shape

(Shading indicates wasted area)

represent the extra area that is gained by a tank of rectangular shape. Remember that this is the area that is gained where the goldfish bowl is at its widest, and at the top (where the bowl is smaller) you will have a much greater area of wasted space, as shown on fig. 3, B.

This question of the water area at the top of the tank is of the greatest importance and that is why it has been emphasized so strongly. More will be said about aquarium tanks in the next chapter, but let us start with one definite rule. **Except for a very short time, no goldfish should be kept in a small, round bowl.**

In addition to its oxygen a fish must have food and it must live under conditions that resemble, as closely as possible, those under

5

which it would live in its natural surroundings. These points are of such importance that they will have to be dealt with in separate chapters, but when looking after fish the following points must be kept in mind.

A fish is a living creature, able to feel fear, discomfort or pain. It is a pet in exactly the same way as a dog, cat, hamster or other land creature. A fish is not capable of learning a wide range of tricks, but it can do simple things such as swimming up for food when a bell is rung, and will even feed from its owner's hand.

So, if you are not prepared to look after your fish and treat them as carefully as you would any other household pet, do not start a fish tank.

2

Setting up a Tank

What kind of a fish tank should you buy?

We have already seen that there is little to be said in favour of the ordinary goldfish bowl. This means that we will almost certainly have to buy a tank of rectangular shape, but these are made in all kinds of sizes and materials.

Some of the smaller tanks are moulded from a sheet of clear plastic. These are very good but the cheaper ones may bulge out and lose their shape under the weight of the water inside, and if an accident should happen it is impossible to mend the tank, which means that a new one has to be bought.

The last remark is also true about tanks of all-glass construction. To stand up to the weight of water that the tanks must hold the glass is often very thick, which may cause it to act like a magnifying glass of poor quality, so that the fish appear distorted.

Unless you stop to work it out it is difficult to realize just how heavy a tank is when it is filled with water, and how important it is that the glass is strong enough to stand up to that weight.

Let us suppose that you have a tank measuring 30 in. long, 12 in. wide and 12 in. deep. We can find out how much water this holds by first calculating how many cubic feet of water it will hold when full, and allowing $6\frac{1}{4}$ gallons of water for each cubic foot.

You know how we find the number of cubic feet in a tank of the size mentioned, so we will write down the sum:

$$\frac{30 \times 12 \times 12}{12 \times 12 \times 12} = 2\frac{1}{2} \text{ cubic feet}$$

As every cubic foot of water is equal to $6\frac{1}{4}$ gallons our tank will hold $15\frac{5}{8}$ gallons of water.

We also know that a gallon of water weighs 10 lb, so the water in a tank of the sizes given will weigh $156\frac{1}{4}$ lb, which is not a great deal less than $1\frac{1}{2}$ cwt.

Having seen how much the water will weigh you may be surprised to know that some tanks are, with the exception of the front glass panel, made entirely of wood. These tanks are perfectly watertight but they are usually more suitable for tropical fish than for ordinary coldwater breeds.

Perhaps the best sort of tank is the one that has a framework made of angle iron, with glass panels on all sides and a bottom that is also of glass but of a heavier and stronger kind than is used for the panels. The glass is bedded into place with 'aquarium cement'.

The only trouble that is likely to occur with a tank of this kind is that if roughly handled the water may leak round the edges of the glass. If this should happen the leak is easily mended with aquarium cement. Should you have an accident and break one of the glass panels you can replace this without having to buy a new tank.

An angle iron tank of the type described is shown in fig. 4.

You can buy your tank from any water-life shop and you will find that they are made in 'standard sizes'. There are several of these. Some of the standard sizes are given below, but there are many others.

Standard sizes, in inches

Length	Breadth	Depth
18	10	10
24	12	12
30	12	12
36	12	16

You will see that in every case the tank has a good surface area that will ensure that there is no shortage of oxygen for the fish living in it.

There is very little chance that you will ever have a fish tank specially made to measurements of your own choosing, but if you should do so, remember that it is **area** and not **depth** that is the most important measurement.

What size of tank should you buy?

To a great extent that will depend on the number and size of the fish that you intend to keep.

8

One 'rule' that is often used is to allow 1 in. of fish (not counting the length of the tail) for every 24 square in. of water surface area. In a tank with surface measurements of 30 in. by 12 in. you could therefore have 15 in. of fish. It does not matter how this 15 in. is divided up. You could have one fish 3 in. long with eight others $1\frac{1}{2}$ in. long, or fifteen fish each 1 in. long, and so on. Remember that these measurements do

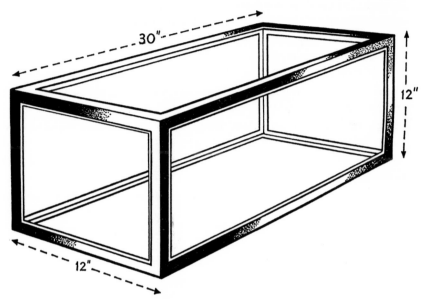

Fig. 4 Recommended tank with 'angle iron' frame and glass panels. This one measures 30 in. x 12 in. x 12 in.

not have to include the length of the caudal fins, and also that as the fish grow one or more will have to be moved to other tanks so that you never have more than 15 in. of fish in the tank.

For a beginner a tank measuring 24 in. by 12 in. by 12 in. (to hold 12 in. of fish) is a useful size. It is not expensive to buy, will hold a fair number of fish, and is easy to keep in good condition.

The next thing to decide is where the tank is to stand, bearing in mind that when filled with water, plus its gravel and plants, it is going to be extremely heavy.

Probably the worst possible place for a tank is directly in front of a window that gets direct sunlight most of the day. It may be that the position of the furniture already in the room will decide where the tank must go. If it must be put in a dark corner it will need to be given some artificial lighting. This is done by buying a metal 'hood' to fit the tank, this hood having a hole to take a lamp-holder that can be connected to the nearest power point.

Before 'setting up' the tank (filling it with water and planting 'aquatics' so that it is ready for the fish) it will be as well to stand the tank in a sink, fill it with water and see if it leaks round the edges of the glass. Very small leaks that start as the water is put in often cure themselves as the increasing weight of the water forces the glass hard against the angle iron framing. More serious leaks will have to be treated with a little aquarium cement, forced into the corners and edges of the frame.

Once you are satisfied that the tank is in order it is 'set up', and this must be done at least five days before the fish are put into it.

What we must aim at when setting up the tank is to make the conditions resemble, as closely as possible, those found in a pond or stream.

A bag of aquarium compost must be bought, put in a bowl, and stood under a running cold water tap for a time to free it of dust and small pieces of rubbish. A layer of washed compost is then put over the base of the aquarium tank, sloping down from a height of between $1\frac{1}{2}$ in. and 2 in. at the back to $\frac{3}{4}$ in. at the front. There is no need to smooth the compost out too evenly, for a few hollows and ridges will make it look more natural.

A few pieces of rockwork may be stood on the compost. Not too much of this should be used, every piece must be placed firmly so that it cannot fall and the pieces should be arranged so that they do not form small 'pockets' in which waterlogged food can be trapped.

Some fish-keepers use pieces of artificial rockwork in the shape of mermaids, wrecked galleons, etc. This is quite in order as long as these items are not made of lime, which can dissolve into the water and gradually poison it. Again, not too much of this artificial rockwork should be used. If natural stone is used it should have no sharp edges, and if it is of the kind that shows layers ('strata') it should be laid in the tank so that the strata are horizontal.

Unless sterilized, natural stones can be responsible for the introduction of undesirable organisms into the tank. It is therefore advisable to pour boiling water over them (or allow them to steep in boiling water) before they are put into the tank.

Fig. 5 Section of completed tank showing compost, rockwork, etc.

Some attempt should be made to have the rockwork looking as natural as possible. Instead of simply placing the stone on the compost, the latter should be slightly heaped round the base of the rocks to make it look as if the stone is thrusting itself up from the bottom of a pond.

A thin layer of coarser aquarium gravel is spread over the compost. Some fish-keepers prefer to use small gaily coloured chips for this, but whichever you choose (chips or gravel) must be rinsed under a tap before being sprinkled into place.

The next step is to half fill the tank with water.

Ordinary tap water is quite suitable, but it is a good idea to fill a pail and let it stand for about twelve hours in the room in which the tank is being set up. This helps to free the water of the slight smell of chlorine that most town supplies have, and will also bring it to the temperature that it should be in the tank.

If the water is simply poured in, it will disturb the gravel and probably leave a bare patch. To avoid this, a large cup is stood on the bottom of the tank and the water poured, **very gently,** into this. As the cup fills, the water will flow down its sides on to the gravel, and once the cup has been completely covered it may be taken away. When the tank is half filled it is ready for stocking with plants that grow under water, these usually being called 'aquatics'.

Fig. 6 Use of cup when filling a tank

There are several reasons for planting aquatics. They help to oxygenate the water and take up certain unwanted gases from it. The fish appreciate the shade and the emergency hiding places that they give, and also find tiny forms of water life on the leaves, which they will eat with delight. Aquatics help to make the tank more like the natural conditions under which the fish live, and, at the same time, make it more attractive in appearance. The plants themselves make use of the manure provided by the fish, and so help to keep the tank clean.

There are several varieties of aquatic plant though not all of them are suitable for coldwater tanks.

A few of the most popular sorts are described below. All can be bought at most water-life stores. In many cases they have a long name in Latin instead of a more common title.

Perhaps the best known of all aquatic plants is *Vallisneria*, sometimes called tape grass. It has long, grass-like leaves of a light green colour and is best planted in small clumps. The special advantages of *Vallisneria* are that it spreads quickly and is one of the best possible plants for producing oxygen. One variety of this particular plant has twisted

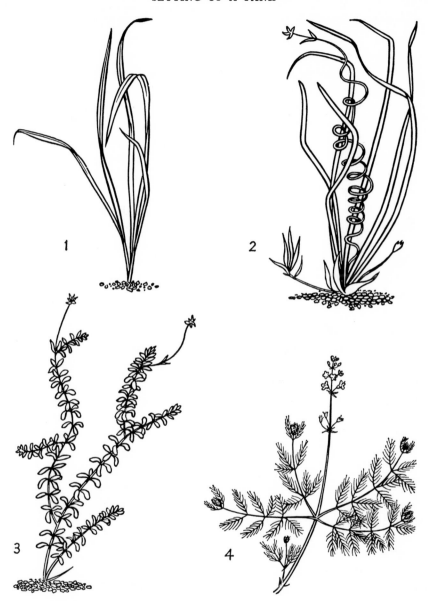

Fig. 7   *1 Vallisneria   2 V. spiralis   3 Elodea   4 Hottonia palustris*

13

leaves which make it look rather more attractive than the plain tape grass.

Elodea, or Canadian water weed, is another excellent oxygenator and is a quick growing species of a dark green colour. It is a favourite plant for the tank or pool in which breeding is to be carried out. The leaves are arranged in whorls around the stem, and are on short stalks. If a small shoot is nipped off and replanted it will root with amazing quickness. In fact, the only disadvantage of this plant is that it needs careful control for if allowed to grow unchecked the tank or pool will soon be crowded out with plant life. It will usually develop much more quickly in a pool than in a tank.

Lagarosiphon is sometimes sold under its old fashioned name of *Elodea crispa*. It is a larger plant than the Canadian water weed and is rather more hardy. While growing quite well in the indoor tank it is usually selected for outdoor pools.

Another useful oxygenating plant is the water violet (*Hottonia*) which looks rather like a miniature pale green fern. It prefers shallow water and in outdoor ponds it will flower attractively. Once the plant has been well established it can be spread by taking cuttings, but each cutting must have tiny rootlets otherwise it cannot possibly live.

These are only a very few of the aquatic plants that can be bought, but when getting plants from a local water-life shop it must be mentioned that they are for a coldwater tank. Some of the more attractive and expensive plants can live only in a warm, tropical tank and to put them in an ordinary goldfish aquarium simply means that they will soon die off and, in fact, be more of a danger than a help to the fish.

Try to choose only healthy-looking, half-grown plants. To get them home from the shop they will have to be wrapped in damp packing or newspaper. They should be planted as soon as possible but not before they have been thoroughly washed in running cold water. Very tiny insect pests, and even disease, can be introduced into a tank by means of its plants, so it is as well to take some care in cleaning them.

Some care should be given to the planting so as to get the best effect. It may help if small clumps of *Vallisneria* are put in the back corners so as to hide the angle iron uprights. The front of the tank should be kept free of plants, while a water violet or similar plant should be given a place of honour where the eye is not distracted from it by other plants crowding close to it. The height to which the plants will grow must also be borne in mind so that attractive varieties are not hidden by taller plants in front.

Planting is best done with the help of a strip of thin, flat wood with a notch cut out of one end.

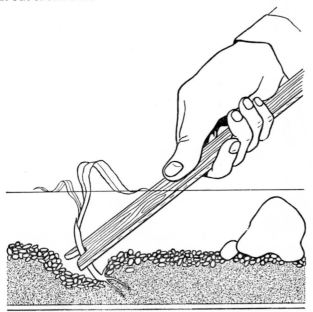

Fig. 8 Notched strip of wood for planting out

A small hole is dug in the gravel and the plant roots are spread out in the loam, the earth and gravel being firmed back over the roots with the end of the stick. The aquatics must be well planted, otherwise they will tend to float away, particularly when more water is added. This can be prevented by putting a lead 'collar' round the bottom of each plant. The collar is simply a narrow strip of lead bent round the plant stem, but it must not be put on so tightly as to affect the growth of the stem.

Fig. 9 Lead collar around stem of plant

Once the plants are firmly and properly in position the tank is topped up with cold tap water. This should be done so that the water is level with the bottom edge of the top horizontal strip of angle iron, for nothing looks worse than to see the top of the water at some inches below the actual top of the tank.

The tank is then given a few days to settle down before the fish are put into it. If it is of the kind that has a hood with an electric light, the lighting can be switched on for about three hours every day, as this will be of some help in getting the plants established.

After a couple of days or so it may be noticed that the water in the tank has gone a delicate shade of green. This is quite natural and nothing to worry about. There is no need to change the water and it will be found that within a few days the water will go back to its original clear state.

The change of colour is brought about by the slightly unnatural conditions in the tank when it is first filled with water. Minute specks of algae develop because of excessive light, and aquatic animal life that can be seen only under a microscope also cause biological and chemical changes in the water. After being undisturbed for a few days the water adjusts itself to the new conditions, the algae die off, the chemical action ceases, and the water clears itself.

Before any mention is made of the fish that will go into the tank something should be said to clear up the question of 'aeration'.

It has already been explained that the fish depend on oxygen to enable them to live, and that this oxygen is absorbed through the water surface in contact with the air.

To increase the amount of oxygen reaching the fish some fish-keepers bubble extra air into the tank with the help of a small electric motor. Usually a 'diffusing stone' is put into the tank to release the air in bubbles of small size, the diffusing block being of natural or artificial stone with holes bored through it on all surfaces. It is connected to the motor by a length of thin rubber piping.

The advantage of artificial aeration is that it allows more fish to be kept in a tank of any particular size, and also makes certain that the oxygen supply is always more than the minimum necessary to keep the fish alive. For the ordinary goldfish tank in which the fish are not overcrowded artificial aeration is quite unnecessary.

Artificial aeration may, in fact, be dangerous on occasion. A number of fish are kept in a tank and, with artificial aeration, are happy enough. If something goes wrong (like the motor breaking down or a power cut that lasts a long time) then there must be a frantic rush round to find another temporary tank for some of the fish.

On the whole, therefore, it is just as well to make do without artificial aeration.

3
Goldfish Breeds

As you probably already know, the goldfish originated in China. The original stock was quite unattractive, being of a dull greenish-olive colour and, in fact, the same variety is still eaten in the East. The young of the domestic goldfish have something of the colour of their wild ancestors, though they soon take on the red, yellow and gold colours with which we are familiar.

We shall never know who first thought of breeding the wild fish so as to produce the handsome species that we have today. In Chinese writings of almost one thousand years ago mention is made of tame goldfish, and they may have been quite common by that date. It is very likely that, when the Chinese poet wrote about them, the only variety that had been domesticated was what we now call the 'common goldfish', but over the centuries the Chinese have produced a great range of fancy varieties. Nowadays, of course, these fish are not necessarily bred only in China.

Although we talk of 'gold' fish, the colour may be red, yellow, very dark, or even mottled.

The choice of goldfish to be kept is largely a personal one, but the beginner should not be too strongly tempted by the appearance of some of the more fancy breeds. A number of these are delicate fish, needing considerable attention and, if kept in a tank with hardier kinds, may soon lose their attractive appearance, particularly if there is an outbreak of tail nipping from any 'bullies' in the tank.

It is better to start with the simpler varieties like the common goldfish and the shubunkin.

All the varieties are different in body shaping and colouring, and may be either scaled or scaleless; the latter are sometimes called 'calico' breeds. The body shapings of some of the best-known varieties have been illustrated in fig. 10 to show the main differences.

When first born the **common goldfish** is almost olive green in colour but it soon darkens until it is almost black. If a specimen is bought as a young fish the blackish markings may still be seen, though by about three months after hatching the fish is showing its proper adult colouring. Although commonly seen only as a small fish the common goldfish can, under good conditions in an outdoor pool, grow to a body length of 9 in. or even more. The common goldfish can live for a considerable number of years and if the tank and other conditions are suitable it will raise young indoors. Most varieties will breed only in an outdoor pool.

A good specimen of the common goldfish has a rather short body, with a smoothly curved back that should show no sign of a hump. The fins should be held fully open but are not particularly large.

The **shubunkin** is one of the more handsome types of goldfish and is a hardy variety that is very popular with beginners. As can be seen from fig. 10, the shaping is easily distinguished from that of the common goldfish by the more exaggerated tail.

The shubunkin does not grow to as large a size as the common goldfish, and is one of the calico (or scaleless) varieties. Such breeds are not really scaleless, but the scales are transparent and more or less too small to be seen. The shubunkin is another variety from which it is comparatively easy to breed.

The range of colourings in the shubunkin is wide, but some of the most expert fish-keepers say that it is only the brighter coloured varieties that should be kept, because the whitish or light pink un-mottled fish are less healthy.

A good specimen of the shubunkin has a blue body colour speckled with black, but also showing patches of brown, red, yellow or even violet.

Fish dealers recognize two different kinds of shubunkin, which they call the 'Bristol' and the 'London'. It is the Bristol shubunkin that is more popular for the indoor tank, while the London shubunkin is considered better for the outdoor pool. The Bristol shubunkin has the better fins while the London variety more closely resembles the common goldfish in body shaping.

Another popular variety is the **comet**. This has the normal goldfish

Fig. 10   *1* Shubunkin   *2* Comet   *3* Telescope-eyed moor   *4* Fantail   *5* Veiltail

colouring, but has a long, slim body with a caudal fin of about the same length as the body. The fins on the underpart of the body are long and pointed.

For the indoor tank the comet is at its best while it is still young. It is a hardy and active fish that needs plenty of space when it is full grown, and so does best in the garden pool. If it is to be bred indoors it needs a fairly large tank and the results are not likely to be as successful with comets as they are with shubunkins. There is an ordinary comet variety as well as a calico breed of many colours.

One of the most attractive of the goldfish breeds is the **fantail.**

This is one of the fancy varieties, having a body that is in the shape of a globe, with two complete caudal fins and double anal fins. While this is a most attractive fish it suffers from the same trouble as all others having a fancy tail, because if it is damaged (either because of an accident or by attack by other fish) the fantail may look very untidy and remain in that state for a long time. A damaged fin will eventually re-grow but may not be completely restored to its original size and shape.

Both calico and scaled varieties of fantail can be bought, the first named being considered better for the indoor tank while the scaled fantail is usually chosen for the garden pond.

The **veiltail** is another breed with both scaled and calico types, and may have either a 'swallowtail' or a 'broadtail'. This breed is even more fanciful than the fantail, and is a most attractive fish when seen moving slowly through the tank. It is not as hardy as most other breeds and does not stand up well to sudden changes of temperature. Some fish-keepers have veiltails in outdoor ponds during the summer, but they must be transferred to an indoor tank for the winter. A veiltail is well worth its place in any tank.

When buying veiltails only young fish should be bought, choosing those in which the tail hangs down in graceful folds. They should be kept in tanks in which there is not too much rockwork on which they may be liable to snag their tails. Most fish-keepers prefer the calico variety of veiltail though it is not quite as hardy as the scaled type.

The five breeds of goldfish described above are the most popular and common with fish-keepers, but there are several other kinds. Once some experience has been gained with the more common types there is a great deal to be said for keeping the rarer breeds, so some notes on these will also be given.

It seems ridiculous to speak of a black 'goldfish', yet that is the colour of the **moor**. A good specimen should be of a dull black colour with no yellow or gold markings. The moor is not a particularly hardy fish (though it will thrive in an indoor tank) and there is no calico variety.

The most noticeable thing about the moor, however, is not the colour but the eyes. These project in a most astonishing way and have been responsible for the fish being known as the 'telescope-eyed moor'. There are also other, but less important breeds of telescope-eyed fish.

Another breed, perhaps even more fantastic, is the **celestial**. With these the projecting eyes are able to look upwards only. This obviously makes life far from easy for the fish, as it can feed only when its food is above it, where it can be seen. It is not a hardy fish, nor even a particularly active one, and apart from its unusual appearance there is little in its favour.

There are many fish-keepers who refuse to buy these very unusual fish, because they feel that there is no excuse for breeding them in such a way, and that they are only freaks. It is not as if such fish are of handsome appearance, for most of them are decidedly ugly, and, to a great extent, such breeds have been spoiled for a natural life. It is true that all goldfish are 'artificial' when compared to the ancestors from which they originated, but most breeds are able to live happily in a way that is not unnatural for a fish.

Sooner or later, however, every fish-keeper comes into contact with these strange breeds, so it is just as well to know something about them.

Although the telescope-eyed moor and the celestial are regarded by many as ugly fish, some breeders have succeeded in making them even more peculiar in appearance.

Fig. 11   *1* Celestial   *2* Goldfish   *3* Lion-head   *4* Oranda

One such variety is the **bubble-eye.** This closely resembles the celestial, but has a large lump under each eye.

Wart-like growths cover the whole head of the **oranda.** This growth should extend over the gill covers in a good specimen of the fish, which usually has a colouring of red and silver. The body shaping is similar to that of the veiltail. The oranda is reasonably hardy but is better kept in a tank than a pool, and if used as a pond fish should certainly be brought indoors during the winter months.

The **lion-head** has been developed from the oranda. With this the warty head is even larger than that of the oranda, but the caudal fin is different, resembling that of the fantail. Another unusual feature is that the variety has no dorsal fin. The lion-head is less hardy than the oranda.

All fancy goldfish are much dearer than the more common species and in some cases (like the oranda and lion-head) are comparatively rare. Against this can be set the point that given average luck a healthy fish may live for more than five years, and that during its lifetime it will not cost a great deal to maintain.

Fish may be bought either at local water-life shops, from local persons having spare fish for sale, or from dealers whose businesses are at some distance from the buyer.

Buying the fish locally means that they can be examined and possibly chosen from a large number of the same variety, so it should be possible to buy healthy-looking stock. There can be little doubt as to whether a fish is healthy or not. It should be of good shape, bright-eyed, active, and with fins held properly. If the fish seems to roll as it swims, or swims at a strange angle with head permanently up or down, it should be rejected for the fish may be suffering from an incurable disease. A couple of minutes spent watching the movements of a fish will tell all that needs to be known about its condition.

Fish bought from a local breeder may be cheaper than those bought from a local shop, but they are often young and may need more careful treatment than older fish bought from a water-life store.

Under no circumstances should fish be bought from a fair-ground or any source in which the dealer is not a proper fish-seller or very interested in the hobby. Fish from such sources are often in poor condition. They may cost little but they prove expensive when they die within a few weeks, and have to be replaced.

There is no great difficulty in moving fish from a local dealer to the new tank.

All that is needed is a fairly large can of water. It must be large enough to give the fish room to be comfortable and be full enough to prevent the water being swirled round too freely. The can must be handled with reasonable care, otherwise the fish may be thrown about violently, and while they may not be severely damaged they may be badly frightened.

Because a can of water weighs heavily, some dealers put the water and fish in a polythene bag. This is satisfactory for the short trip from the shop to the new tank, but there is a point to be watched. Such a bag should always be carried, for if it is stood on the floor of a car, for example, the bottom will spread out under the weight of the water, and the depth be made so shallow that the fish are put to some distress.

Obtaining fish from a dealer at some distance from the buyer is a rather different matter. This should be done only when there is a strong reason for it, and usually the beginner at fish-keeping will find that all he or she needs can be bought locally.

There is usually no need to worry about the condition of stock bought by post, as most advertisers are honest men who stand to lose far more than they gain by selling fish of poor quality. The fish are usually sent by passenger train which has to be met at the local station, so it will be seen that buying by post can be expensive. Goldfish that have made a long train journey often seem dispirited and out of sorts when first received, but they soon perk up again.

In general, goldfish are healthy creatures but they may suffer from certain illnesses. Some of these are highly contagious and may spread quickly from fish to fish. Even worse, some of the illnesses are fatal.

Once a tank has been set up for some time no newly bought fish should be put in it until after an isolation period of seven days. If any disease is present in the new stock it should show itself before the isolation period is over.

The isolation tank does not need to be anything elaborate. It may be covered with gravel on the base but as long as it is not stood on a window ledge in direct sunlight it need not be planted with aquatics.

When setting up a tank for the first time the fish may, of course, be put direct into the main tank without a period of isolation, for in the dealer's shop they will have been in contact long enough for any damage to be done. However, with a newly started tank there is no need to be too gloomy as regards the health of the fish.

The stock must be put into the tank gently. The easiest way of doing this is to hold the container under water, open it, and allow the fish to swim out gently.

More about the feeding of fish will be said later but it may be pointed out that a fish should not be fed as soon as it is put into its new tank. For one thing, it may be rather too frightened to take food, so it should be given at least twelve hours to get used to its new home before any food is given. There is no need to worry about the fish getting hungry over this period. They do not need as much food as might be thought, and they find more than enough very tiny forms of animal life in the water to satisfy them for several days if necessary.

Some fish-keepers put snails and other forms of water life in the tank but this is not, usually, a good thing. Water snails eat a certain amount of waste food but, of course, they also excrete waste and on balance they will probably make more waste than they clean up. They also breed extremely quickly and use a certain amount of the oxygen that is essential to the life of the fish. It is not always easy to see that one or more snails have died, and their rotting bodies may be poisoning the water more quickly than an equal quantity of un-eaten food. Nor do they look attractive on the glass or plants. Unless the numbers can be kept under control water snails are best kept in the outdoor pool rather than in a tank.

Other forms of life, such as pond mussels, are also out of place in an indoor aquarium, as they are likely to uproot the plants by burrowing or need too much oxygen.

Not everybody will want to keep goldfish and there are other cold-water breeds that can be kept successfully in an aquarium. Some breeds will live quite happily with goldfish while others need to be kept only with their own kind.

More coldwater breeds are described in the next chapter, but the remarks above about buying and transporting goldfish apply equally well to other coldwater breeds, which must be kept in a tank set up with plants and gravel as already described.

4

Other Coldwater Breeds

One well-known coldwater fish that thrives in an indoor tank and is no trouble to catch is the ordinary **stickleback**. This is the fish often called the 'tiddler'.

It might be thought that the stickleback is of little interest to anybody who takes fish-keeping seriously, but this is not true. In a well kept tank they are lively and active, and for those interested in the breeding of fish they are unusual as they are true nest builders. The main drawback with them is that they are a quarrelsome lot and can keep an aquarium tank in a constant state of panic unless it is confined to sticklebacks, and even then trouble between the males can be expected on occasions.

The sticklebacks cannot be fed on dried foods and although they will accept a certain amount of scraped, raw liver, etc., they are best fed on live food. They have extremely small mouths and micro-worms will therefore prove the most suitable for them.

There are two varieties of stickleback, the 'three-spined' and the 'ten-spined', the latter being much the rarer of the two. The first-named may have two, three or four separate spines on the front of the dorsal fin. The ordinary colour is a brownish-green, rather lighter on the underside of the body, but in the spring the male puts on his 'mating colour', which is reddish underneath and greenish above. The stickleback is easily caught in freshwater ponds and streams.

The breed rarely grows to a length greater than 2 in., but because of its speed and energy it should never be kept in an aquarium with a length of less than 2 ft.

Another very common fish that can be netted in running water, and less frequently in freshwater pools is the **minnow**.

The breed does not grow to any great size but is not afraid of larger fish, and is particularly active. In a way, it is rather a 'pirate', swooping down and snatching food almost from the mouths of fish twice its size. It is not happy when kept as a single specimen and needs to be one of a shoal of about half a dozen.

The general colour of the fish is brownish merging into areas of a dark green, but during the breeding season the males take on some patches of very brilliant colour.

To keep the bottom of the tank free of food, some fish-keepers put one or more **catfish** in the tank. These feed at the bottom of the aquarium and so get the food that has not been taken by the goldfish at higher water levels. Unfortunately, catfish are not of attractive appearance or colouring and most of them develop into 'tail nippers' so that they cannot be put into the same tank as veiltails or fantails.

Cold water 'cats' are imported from North America and are usually difficult to obtain locally. They are given various descriptions, such as 'black', 'spotted', and so on, but it is sometimes found that the same name is given, by different dealers, to different breeds. The catfish cannot really be recommended for the small indoor aquarium and it has only been mentioned here to complete the record of fish that may be suggested by a dealer as being suitable for a tank.

A rather better scavenger is the **gudgeon,** for this breed also lives and feeds towards the bottom of the tank. It has a mixed colouring of brown, blue and green, and is capable of growing to a length of 6 in., though this is only likely to occur with fish kept in a pool.

In appearance **bitterling** are among the most attractive of the ordinary coldwater breeds and they have the advantage, for an indoor tank, that they do not grow too large, 3 in. being about their maximum size.

As is the case with nearly all breeds, the females are not particularly striking, being olive-green and silvery in colour, but the male is a much more handsome creature, having a mauve and pinkish or greenish body, with red fins; the latter have a thin edging of black. This particular fish is of great interest to fish-breeders for, as is shown in a later chapter, it is not a difficult fish from which to breed in an indoor tank, and it has a most unusual way of raising its young.

For hobbyists who intend to keep fish in an outdoor pool small specimens of **dace** are worth considering. They are rather slender

PLATE 1 (*Above*) Goldfish
(*Below*) A pair of bitterling with the painter's mussel in which the female deposits her eggs

PLATE 2

Four stages in making a garden pool:

Hole prepared for pool. (Note ledges left for aquatic plants)

Hole covered with special sheeting and weighted along the edges

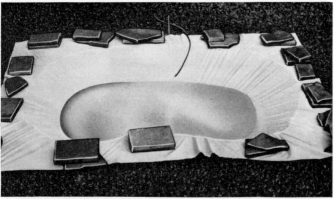

Pool partially filled by means of a hose-pipe (Note polythene material adjusting to shape of pool)

Completed pool with slabbed surround

(*Left*) The native white water-lily

(*Below*) Water-lily (*Nymphaea tuberosa richardsoni*) with splendid white blooms and conspicuous green sepals

PLATE 3 (*Below*) An attractive garden pond in summer

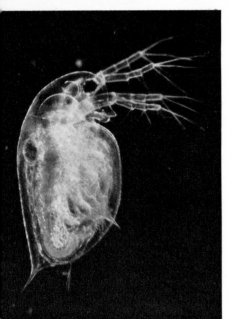

PLATE 4: (*Top*) Mosquito larvae and pupae at the surface of the water (magnified)
(*Below left*) Water flea (*Daphnia*) (magnified)
(*Below right*) Fish louse (*Argulus*). Actual size ¼ in.

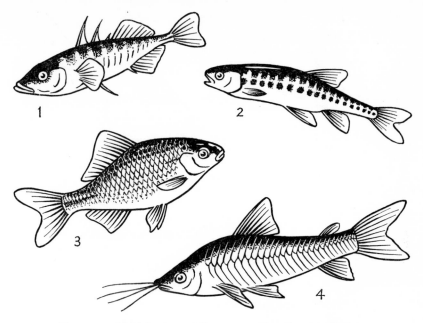

Fig. 12 *1* Stickleback *2* Minnow *3* Bitterling *4* Catfish

fish of a silvery colour. Dace always draw attention to the pool because of the way in which they break the surface in search of flies and other small insects.

Another species that keeps close to the surface in search of flies is the **golden orfe**. Again, except as a very young specimen, it is a fish more for the pool than the indoor tank, but as a pond fish it has the great advantage that it keeps close to the surface and is always easy to see.

The golden orfe is a slim fish of a pale yellow colour with silver beneath, though the older specimens may develop black markings. It is extremely active but in very hot weather larger fish of the breed show some distress if not kept in a pool of good size. This is to be expected of all fish whose natural home is in running water.

The carp is a coldwater breed but is of poor natural colouring. It is the original type from which the goldfish was developed so that

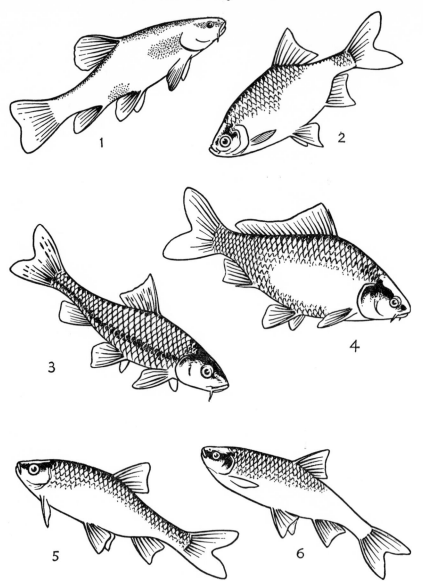

Fig. 13 *1* Golden tench *2* Golden rudd *3* Gudgeon *4* Hi-goi carp
5 Golden orfe *6* Dace

there was, for a long time, no attempt to breed another special form of carp for the aquarium tank or pool.

During the past few years, however, the **hi-goi** carp has become popular, though this is a pond rather than an aquarium fish.

This breed can be red or yellow in colour, is deep bodied and has very prominent scales. While small specimens can be kept in a tank the breed will, under good conditions, grow to a body length of 12 in. or more, so while many hobbyists delight in owning one or more specimens it is not the kind of fish that can be kept by all.

The **golden rudd** is another fish that can be kept in a tank when small and in a pool when more mature. It is one of the slender type of fish, with a golden-red body colouring and bright red fins. The golden rudd is noted for its activeness.

There are two varieties of tench but the more popular is the **golden tench.** This breed is one that feeds from the bottom and prefers live to dried foods. It is like the rudd in that only the smaller specimens can be kept in an indoor tank. The colour of the young fish is of a golden yellow shade, but the colour may darken with age. Even young tench can look quite big when compared to young goldfish, but they are peaceful and cause no trouble in the tank.

When coldwater breeds other than goldfish are bought it is always advisable to buy them in pairs. They live peacefully with goldfish as a general rule, but they are always happier when they are with at least one of their own kind.

5

Feeding the Fish

It will be appreciated that, as well as oxygen, a fish must have food, not only to keep it alive but also in good health.

Most beginners make two mistakes in feeding fish. The first is to give the fish far too much food at any one time, and the second is to supply the same kind of food at every meal.

It is quite wrong to think that fish are constantly eating. Most of the breeds have very small appetites and however much food there may be in the tank, they will ignore it as soon as their appetites are satisfied. There may be one or two individual fish who overeat (and suffer digestive troubles as a result) but this is uncommon. What happens is that the unwanted food falls to the bottom of the tank, rots, and gives off gases that tend to poison the water and so harm the fish.

Similarly, if a fish is given the same kind of food at every meal it certainly will not starve, but it will be about as happy as a human being who had to live on nothing but bread and water. While fish do not need the numerous changes of diet that humans enjoy, they will be healthier and more contented if the meals show a little variety.

A fish is a cold-blooded creature with a body temperature that is the same as that of the water in which it is living; the amount of food needed by the fish to keep it active and in good health depends on the water temperature. The colder the water the less food needed, but there is also an upper limit at which it could almost be described as 'too hot for eating'.

The fish's appetite (which, as stated, is never very large) is thus affected by temperature, and during the spring and early summer months it will need more food than during the winter.

Most coldwater fish are 'omnivorous', which means that they will eat food of either vegetable or animal origin, though some breeds prefer one kind to the other.

As far as the fish-keeper is concerned food can be divided into two kinds, 'dried' and 'live'.

The first may consist of such foods as dried shrimp or dried daphnia, and is usually taken as meaning the powdered diets sold by the makers of pet foods. These foods are sold in cans and packets of different sizes.

Every maker of pet foods works to his own formula to provide a food that is scientifically based to give the fish a proper 'balanced' diet. If made by one of the well-known firms the food can be relied on as being fresh and suitable for the breeds for which it is sold. To human eyes two tins of dried food from different manufacturers will look identical, but the fish will be able to distinguish them. Some variety in the diet can therefore be brought about by feeding alternately dried foods from two different makers.

It is probably better to buy the smaller sized containers of food as it will keep fresher, as long as the lid is replaced after food has been taken from the packet. Dried food must never be handled with wet fingers, as some of the food left in the container is certain to get damp and may start to rot. This may not be noticeable while the food is in the packet but it will be very slightly 'off' when given to the fish, and this is not a good thing.

Most fish go for the largest sized pieces of food that their gullets can manage, but they cannot tear at food like a dog. On the other hand they will ignore very small food grains that therefore sink to the bottom of the tank and rot.

Packaged foods contain grains of mixed sizes. This will not greatly matter when the fish in a tank are of different sizes, for the small grains ignored by the larger fish will be taken by the smaller specimens.

When necessary the food should be put through a sieve. Any fine food dust that may be sifted out can be thrown away, unless it is of a size small enough for any 'fry' or very young fish in the tank.

One rule that must be followed is that the fish should never be given more food at one time than they can eat in five minutes.

One of the cleanest ways of giving dried foods is to make use of a 'feeding ring'. This is a fairly large plastic ring which is usually anchored to the side of the tank by a rubber sucker. The dry food is sprinkled inside the ring which helps to keep it in the one area, and although sooner or later the food will get waterlogged and fall, it will do so over a small area and can then be removed quite easily with a dip tube.

Fig. 14 Feeding ring anchored to tank

Some beginners damp the dried food immediately before putting it in the tank, but this is the wrong thing to do. If the food is already wet it will fall to the bottom almost immediately, whereas dry food will take longer to sink, according to the time that it takes to soak through. Many fish prefer to swoop at their food as it falls through the water, and it is better to have a small trickle of food falling towards the bottom of the tank than to have the entire feed sinking at once.

When feeding, about one-quarter of the proposed meal should be sprinkled into the feeding ring. If the fish eat this the rest of the meal may be sprinkled in, but if they ignore the first sprinkling it is proof that they are not hungry and the rest of the food should be withheld.

34

The fish should be fed, as far as possible, at the same time every day and from the same area of the tank (this will be easy if a feeding ring is used). It is amusing to see how quickly the fish get to know their meal time and how they join the lunch queue just before it is due to be served.

As already explained, food requirements are largely a matter of temperature. An aquarium tank is kept indoors where the temperature is much the same all the year round. The feeding of pond fish is dealt with in another chapter, but for aquarium stock one meal only should be given each day. On the other hand, aquarium fish do not have a true 'winter' so feeding will have to be kept up all the year round.

Live food has one great advantage in that it does not rot if not eaten immediately it is put in the tank, and it is kept alive by such a small amount of oxygen that its presence does not affect the fish.

Perhaps the best-known live food is 'daphnia', which is sometimes known as the 'water flea'. This is, of course, in no way related to the true flea but is so called because of the way in which it moves jerkily through the water. Daphnia are to be found in nearly all ponds, streams, and even ditches.

Armed with a net, most fish-keepers would be able to collect daphnia from local pools, but this is not a wise thing to do. Daphnia bred naturally usually come from slightly contaminated water and carry tiny parasites that are dangerous to fish life. Live food caught by the fish-keeper himself is a common way of introducing illness into the aquarium tank.

Almost every dealer in water-life sells live daphnia. These will have been bred under safe conditions in porcelain tanks, and the hobbyist should always use such daphnia in preference to catching his own.

Anybody with an uncovered rainwater butt near the house will know what the larvae of mosquitoes looks like. They are tiny creatures, about $\frac{1}{4}$ in. long, and rather similar to tadpoles in the way that they are constantly wriggling. Adult goldfish enjoy a meal of mosquito larvae, though young fish may find them too large to swallow. The mosquito eggs from which the larvae hatch out

35

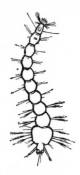

Fig. 15
Mosquito larva
(enlarged)

resemble clusters of small black grains, and if these are recognized they may be kept in a suitable can of water until the larvae hatch.

The earthworm is usually too large to be fed to fish whole except, occasionally, to large pond-bred varieties. To form an animal diet they may be chopped into small pieces or ground between the plates of a 'worm shredder' that can be bought at any water-life shop.

Many hobbyists dislike the job of preparing earthworms and find that 'tubifex' or 'micro-worms' are appreciated by the fish and are cleaner and easier to serve as food.

Tubifex worms are very thin, from 1 in. to 1½ in. long and red in colour. Under natural conditions they live in the mud of slow moving tidal rivers, and are on sale regularly in most water-life shops.

Before being put into a tank these creatures should be placed in a glass container under a slowly dripping water tap, the water being changed from time to time. Treated in this way for some hours, they will be thoroughly clean before being fed to the fish, and there will be less chance of tiny parasites being introduced into the tank. Tubifex worms treated in the way described can be kept alive for several days. It is best to feed the worms to the stock in numbers that are quickly eaten.

Fish-keepers living some distance from a town may find it impossible to buy the tubifex worms across a shop counter. This does not create a great difficulty as there are many firms that supply live food by post, and it is possible to have a permanent order so that a certain quantity of food is posted at regular intervals.

A live food that will be taken by fish of all sizes, including quite young fry, is known as 'micro-worm'. These worms are very tiny in size, white in colour, and usually cultivated by the fish-keeper himself.

This is not as messy as might be thought.

Breeding is done in small glass jars, and four or five of these should be started at intervals of two to three days so that a fresh batch of micro-worms are ready for feeding to the fish at regular intervals. These cultures must be used in proper order, so each jar should be labelled to show the date on which the culture was started. Once cultures have been started and the worms are being 'harvested' the process can be kept on almost indefinitely.

The 'starting culture' for the worms has to be bought, but is quite cheap.

Fig. 16 Date-labelled jars for breeding micro-worms

When the time has come to start a culture a spoonful of thin oatmeal porridge is put at the bottom of one of the jars and allowed to cool. A drop of the starting culture is then put into it. This process is repeated with the other jars at the required intervals.

After a couple of days the surface of the porridge will be in constant movement because of the masses of worms in it, though each worm is too small to be seen with the naked eye.

Once the culture has reached this state the question arises as to how to get the worms into the tank. To put any of the porridge in the aquarium is not the proper answer, for although the fish will get some of the worms the porridge itself will start to make the water foul.

To collect the worms a few headless matchsticks are soaked in cold water. Some of these are laid on the porridge, with a second layer across so as to bridge them. Within a few days a great number of

37

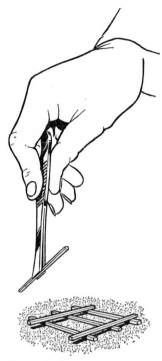

Fig. 17 Collecting micro-worms

micro-worms will have worked their way up on to the top layer of matchsticks. These, in turn, can be lifted up with tweezers and rinsed off into the tank.

By using each jar in turn a good and regular supply of micro-worms is made available, but the time must come when the jar is seen to be drying up, and mould may even form on the porridge.

When this happens an entirely fresh mixture of porridge must be made and put into a clean jar, and a very small quantity of the porridge from an old jar is put into it to start the new culture. It is best to dispose of the old jars.

Like micro-worms, 'white worms' are particularly suitable for feeding during the winter months when it may be difficult to obtain other forms of live food.

Again, the worms have to be bred by the fish-keeper, and the culture has to be set up three weeks before the first batch of worms is wanted. It is advisable to set up a series of containers that are 'seeded' at intervals of several days.

The worms breed most readily in a mixture of equal quantities of leaf mould and peat.

This mixture should be put in a container to a depth of 2 in. to 2½ in. The container must be secure at the edges and along the bottom, or the worms will soon escape. A metal or glass container made in one piece will be the most suitable kind of thing.

The worms have to be fed. Oatmeal porridge is a suitable diet but a food that seems to be particularly favoured by the worms is stale white bread soaked in milk. The bread should be cut into small cubes.

Small pockets are made in the soil and a little of the culture (which may be bought from a water-life store) is put in each feeding area.

Cultures thrive if they are kept in the dark at a temperature of about 55° to 65°F, which means that they will not do well, for example, if kept in a draughty outdoor shed in winter. The container can be covered with a piece of glass or damp sacking which will help to keep the worm in bounds and also prevent rapid drying out of the soil in which they are breeding.

If glass is used to cover the culture a number of the adult worms will gather on the underside of this, and can then be swept into the tank quite easily. Another good way of trapping the worms is to lay some bread on top of the soil to serve as bait, for after a while it will be found that the worms have gathered under it.

White worms should be washed free of the earth in which they have grown. They are large enough to be handled with a pair of tweezers, and a bunch of them can be rinsed in a jar of water without any trouble.

Fig. 18 White worms, showing cross-section of soil with feeding areas of bread cubes

When live food is in short supply, or for a change of diet, raw liver or beef can be fed to the fish.

It is not possible to chop this up finely enough, but the meat can be scraped off with a knife so that it is served in a pulpy state. There are other kinds of raw meat that can be given in the same way, though pork and other fatty foods should be avoided.

It may be noticed that some varieties of fish are continuously nibbling the leaves of aquatic plants. These fish are those that like a high vegetable content in their food and if this is missing they get it from the plants. Some fish-keepers occasionally chop up a small piece of fresh lettuce and put this in the tank.

It always pays to study the likes and dislikes of the fish in any particular tank, and to adjust the diet accordingly.

The rules for the feeding of fish are, however, very simple. They are: (1) do not give too much food at one time; (2) feed regularly but only one meal per day; (3) put some variety into the diet.

6

The Maintenance of a Fish Tank

There is more to keeping fish than putting them in a well planted tank and feeding them. The necessary care of the tank and its fish is called 'maintenance'.

It is true to say that the time spent on maintenance is little, yet if neglected the fish will suffer and the tank, instead of being an attractive item, will become a messy, foul-smelling piece of equipment.

When a tank has been in use for some time it is said to have 'aged' or 'matured'. When this happens the water will have changed colour slightly, there will be tiny growths on the rockwork, and the whole tank will have a much more natural appearance than when it was first set up. This, of course, is all to the good.

After a while what appears to be a kind of fungus may start growing on the inside of the tank. This is a form of minute plant life called an 'alga' or, in the plural, 'algae'. It is perfectly harmless and, in fact, the fish will be seen nibbling at it, but if there is a great deal of it the tank begins to look untidy.

There are different types of algae, some being of a bright green colour and others a rather dull brown.

The growth of an alga depends on the amount of light reaching the tank. The formation of a brown alga is encouraged by insufficient light and a green alga by too much light. By moving the tank to a position where the lighting conditions are correct, algae will cease to form in an indoor tank.

Algae in reasonable quantities help towards making the tank look natural, and many fish-keepers like to see a thin layer of green algae on the back panel of the tank. On the ends and front panel the algae hide the fish from view and once a week or so (according to how fast they grow) the algae must be removed.

The algae are scraped off the sides so that they fall to the bottom of the tank; this must be done with as little disturbance to the fish as

41

possible. Special plastic scrapers are sold for the job but it can be done equally well with a razor blade fastened at the end of a strip of wood, or with an old dinner knife.

Although the scraping will clean the sides it only puts the algae on the bottom of the tank, which still looks untidy. There may also be scraps of food and other rubbish at the bottom of the tank, but note that fish manure is not rubbish as it is needed to fertilize the plants.

The simplest method of clearing the rubbish is to siphon it away.

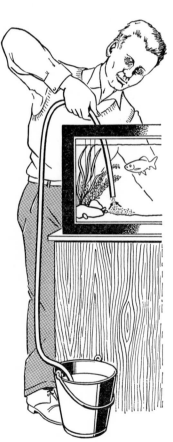

A drawing of the siphoning equipment has been given here.

It consists of a rubber tube long enough to reach from the bottom of the tank to a pail standing on the floor; the tube can be of $\frac{1}{2}$ in. bore. One end of the tube is put in the tank and the air is sucked out of it until water starts to flow through. The water will continue to flow as long as the end of the tube is kept under water, but the bottom of it should be moved gently over the gravel so as to take up the rubbish with the water.

Once the tank has been cleaned in this way it will have to be topped up with fresh cold tap water. This water should be of approximately the same temperature as that siphoned out of the tank. Some hours before siphoning off the rubbish, therefore, some water should be run off into a basin and stood in the room in which the tank is installed so that the water has a good chance to get to room temperature.

Fig. 19 Siphoning out the debris

When there is not much rubbish

to be taken out or for cleaning up unwanted food only, a 'dip tube' can be used.

This is simply a piece of glass tubing of about $\frac{1}{2}$ in. diameter. One end of this tube is kept closed by putting the thumb over it, and the other end is put into the tank just above the rubbish to be removed. On lifting the thumb some of the water and rubbish will be forced into the tube. When the latter has been closed again by putting the thumb over the top of it, it can be lifted free of the tank and the water and rubbish dropped into a bucket merely by taking the thumb off the top of the tube.

It will be seen that a dip tube takes far less water from the tank than does siphoning, but it is an excellent way of picking up small pieces of rubbish. Even so, the tank will have to be topped up sooner or later, and when this is done water of a temperature similar to that taken from the tank should be used.

This last point is really important.

It may sound ridiculous to talk of a goldfish catching a chill, but in some respects this is what happens if it undergoes a sharp change of temperature. A drop of one or two degrees Fahrenheit does not matter greatly, but a severe change of temperature (unless it occurs very gradually) cannot do anything but harm to the fish.

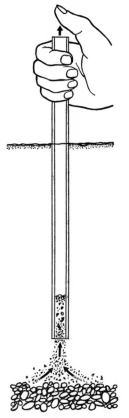

Fig. 20 Using the dip tube

One of the greatest dangers to fish can be poisonous gases resulting from food decaying in the tank. That is why it is always emphasized that fish should be given only as much food as they will clear up in a few minutes. Uneaten food falls to the bottom of the tank, often works itself under a rock or among the gravel, and steadily rots. It is not long before the danger level is reached and fish begin to die. That is why the routine cleaning of the tank is so important.

When a tank has been in use for some time it may be found that water is leaking round the edges and that the metalwork frame is going rusty. It is then time for a thorough clean up, for once such conditions have started they can develop quickly and lead to serious trouble.

The fish have to be moved to other quarters and it is on occasions such as this that a spare tank can be so valuable.

The areas where leakage is occurring should be marked in pencil on the outside of the tank, which is then emptied. The cement round the areas of leakage should be raked out with a thin-bladed knife or bradawl, and fresh 'aquarium cement' worked into place with the same kind of tool; a thin bead of the cement can be left down the inside edge of the angle. The glass must be held firmly as the cementing is done, though later the water pressure will bed the glass down firmly.

Any rust on the metalwork must be chipped off and two coats of cellulose paint or enamel put on. This paintwork must dry properly before the tank is set up again.

When the fish are fed almost completely on dried foods it is advisable to put a small pinch of Epsom salts in the tank at intervals of a month. If this is not done the fish may get constipated, which can lead to more serious troubles.

Many fish-keepers believe that most of the illnesses affecting fish are the fault of their owner because of poor maintenance of the tank.

It is certainly true that 'black sand' (or 'foul sand' as it is sometimes called) may create conditions favourable to the spread of disease.

If a poorly kept tank is examined patches of slightly discoloured gravel may be seen, with what appear to be cobwebs on the surface. When the sand is disturbed it will be seen to be absolutely black under the top layer, and to have a most disgusting smell. This is 'black sand' and has been caused by the rotting of food in that area. If the sand had been left undisturbed bubbles of poisonous gas would have forced themselves up through the water, the more delicate of the fish would have been killed off and the stronger ones badly affected.

In the tank that is cleaned properly and regularly, black sand will not develop. If the tell-tale cobweb signs are noticed the sand that they cover must be lifted out with a big siphon tube. Clean sand to make good the deficiency can then be trickled through a tube to the bottom of the tank, being raked level with a table fork. In the case of severe attack it will be found easier to transfer the fish and plants elsewhere, disposing of the foul sand and sterilizing the tank with hot water.

Another trouble that may occur is 'milky water' and the very name explains the appearance of the affected tank.

This, again, is caused by rotting food, but usually occurs in a newly set up tank. Perhaps the best way to deal with the trouble is to stop supplying food for twenty-four hours and to cut down the quantity of rations supplied.

Half the milky water should be siphoned off and replaced with water of the same temperature, this being done as soon as the condition is noticed. If the milky water has not cleared within a couple of days the siphoning and refilling can be repeated.

A new tank takes some time to settle down and the appearance of the water may change from day to day until the tank is fully aged. There is no need to worry about this, or to keep changing the water unless there is definite trouble from rotting food.

Carelessness in re-topping the tank leads to the plants and gravel being disturbed.

To avoid this a small piece of wood may be floated in the tank, and the water poured gently on to this. During re-topping some dust and dirt may float up to the surface and this can be skimmed off on a piece of newspaper or sheet polythene.

The hobbyist should always stop people tapping on the tank 'to attract the attention of the fish'. This tapping sets up sound waves which can be irritating (and, sometimes, even dangerous) to the fish. Similarly, nobody should be allowed to put a hand inside the tank unless it is absolutely necessary, for this also frightens the fish.

If fish have to be netted it will be found easier to do if one large and one small net are used simultaneously. The fish should be driven into the larger net with the smaller, and should not be scooped up from beneath. The fish may well be lifted but some may jump clear of the net and even out of the tank when the net breaks the surface of the water. A square, rather than a round net, will be found the more handy, as there is less chance of the fish escaping at the edges of the net.

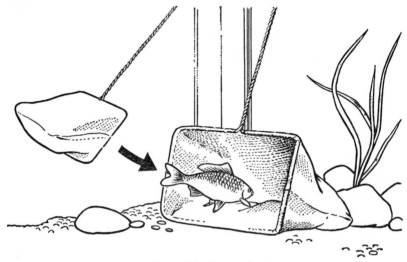

Fig. 21 Netting method

In general, fish will keep healthier if the lighting is reduced during the winter months. This may be done either by reducing the hours during which the lighting is on or by using bulbs of lower wattage.

Some fish-keepers have the tank lighted almost continuously. There is no evidence that this harms the fish, though it does make the conditions unnatural. On the other hand, it has been proved that young fish develop more steadily if the lights are switched off to give them a fairly long 'night'.

Certain equipment is used for netting and handling sick fish, and the possibility of introducing disease into the tank by means of contaminated equipment must not be overlooked.

This applies particularly to the fish net. A small net should always be reserved for the handling of such stock. Once the fish has been cured and replaced in the main tank the net should be boiled to sterilize it.

The problem of feeding the fish and maintaining the tank during a holiday period often puzzles the beginner.

The first point to remember is that in a well established tank adult fish can last two to three weeks without being fed, and will suffer no ill effects.

For the ordinary week-end holiday there is no problem. A normal meal is given at the usual time when going away and the same after the return home. It is natural to want to make these feeds larger than usual, but this should not be done. For a short period such as this the lighting can be kept on.

If it is necessary to leave for a longer period than this (say, for about five days) the light bulbs should be replaced with some of a lower wattage.

If away for more than three weeks it might be possible to find an experienced friend who will look after the fish. If not, an inexperienced friend could be asked to do the job if (a) all the meals are done up in individual packets, and (b) it is made clear that only one meal per day is to be given, and if he cannot feed the fish on any one day they must miss the meal and not be given double rations at any time. The packaging of dry food is a simple enough matter, and live food can be done up in small plastic bags or containers.

Even with clear instructions such as this it is quite likely that the tank will be rather messy as regards uneaten food (and possibly algae) at the end of a long holiday, and once back the work of putting things right should not be too long delayed.

7

The Garden Pond

Many fish-keepers are surprised when it is suggested that they keep a garden pool, believing it is expensive to build and difficult to look after.

This is not true. It is possible to make a simple pool for considerably less than £3 and it is no more difficult to maintain a pool than to look after an indoor tank.

One point must be noted. Most fancy goldfish are not hardy enough to be kept in an outdoor pool, especially during the winter months. It is safer to rely on the common goldfish or shubunkin for stocking the pond.

There are two main types of pool, the 'informal' and the 'formal'.

Most hobbyists will be more interested in the informal pool which is small, has an irregular outline, and is particularly well suited for a

Fig. 22 An informal pool

48

small garden. The formal pool is usually much larger, circular or rectangular in plan (possibly with paving round the edges) and is usually built of concrete or brickwork. The informal pool is usually of materials that are easier to handle.

The simplest of all informal pools is the one lined with polythene sheet, and it costs very little to make.

The first step is to dig a hole the shape and depth of the pool. In plan it should be of an irregular shape and, as shown on the drawing, a step should be left round the edges so that aquatic plants can later be set out.

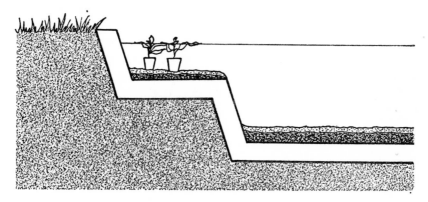

Fig. 23 Step in concrete pool

The pool is lined with a sheet of 500 gauge polythene; this is fairly thick. Whatever the shape of the pool, the polythene will be pressed into close contact with the earth by the pressure of the water, but it is necessary to arrange that when the pool is filled the edges of the polythene must overlap the earth by about 12 in. on all edges. Rockwork covering this overlap will hold the edges of the polythene sheet firmly in place, and if small pockets of earth are arranged in the rockwork, alpines and similar plants can be set out to make the pool look even more attractive.

Such a pool will last for years (though it is not the easiest type to empty and clean), but there must be no sharp flints or stones in the earth walls of the pool, as, under the pressure of water, these may cut the polythene.

When planning any pool it should, if possible, be sited at the lowest part of the garden, for this is where water would gather naturally. Another important point is that the pond should not be in a position where dead leaves can be blown into it, and this means that it must be sited well away from trees and hedges that shed their leaves in the winter.

Another kind of informal pool is made in prefabricated glass fibre.

These cost more than the polythene sheet pools mentioned above, but can be bought in a good range of shapes and sizes. All that has to be done with these is to dig a hole of the proper size and shape, and drop the pool into place. Steps for aquatic plants are already formed in the sides of the pool, but again care must be taken to see that there are no sharp stones between the earth and the fibre glass.

Another simple kind of informal pool can be made by sinking a zinc bath or cistern into the ground. The straight edges at the top of these can be broken up with a few pieces of stonework overlapping the edges so that the shape does not seem too regular. Before a cistern or bath can be used in this way it must be painted inside and out, with a few coats of thin bitumastic paint, and must then be filled,

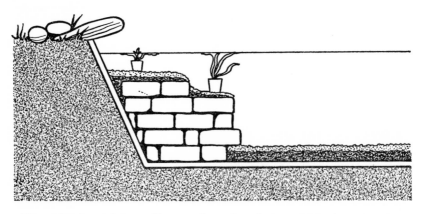

Fig. 24 Bricks used for making step in pool made from old bath, cistern, etc.

allowed to stand for a day, emptied and then refilled, several times before it is safe to use either for fish or plants.

Second-hand baths and tanks are easy to get hold of and reasonably cheap. Next to the use of polythene sheet this is the cheapest way of making an informal pool but it is necessary to have some form of step for the aquatic plants. This can usually be arranged by standing a few bricks in place.

The building of a pool in concrete is such a big and expensive job that anybody who wishes to do it should read one of the specialized books on the subject.

Good quality loam is spread over the bottom of the pool, and also the top of the steps, and a layer of coarse washed sand is put over the loam. The loam should be put to a depth of 4 in., and the sand to about 2 in.

To avoid disturbing the sand and loam a large bucket can be stood in the centre of the pond and the water trickled gently into it. Once the bucket is filled the water will overflow the sides and start to fill the pond. When the latter is half full the bucket can be removed.

One of the advantages of a pool is the chance it gives to do something really attractive in the way of aquatic plants.

The best time for planting is the early spring but they may be set out at any time until the early autumn, as long as they are well rooted. They may be planted direct into the loam, but in some cases it might be better to leave them in their pots, standing these either on the step or on the bottom of the pool, according to the depth of water they need.

There are far too many aquatic plants to advise which particular species should be chosen. Perhaps the best idea is to study the advertisements in magazines that deal with water-life and also the catalogues that can be obtained without a great deal of trouble. These will list the different varieties that can be bought, describe their needs as regards depth of water, and so on, and the size and colour of the flower. This should make the selection of some suitable plants much easier.

It is always useful to have a 'centre piece' in the pool, because this is not only an attractive feature but also makes a shady lurking place for the fish on summer days.

The favourite plant for this purpose is the water-lily, but some grow so strongly that they are not suitable for a small pool though they will thrive in a large pond. The persons who sell the lilies are always ready to give advice as to which varieties to choose if they are told the size of the pool and the depth of the water. Water-lilies are grown from rhizomes, which can be divided in the spring.

Fig. 25 Water-lilies

Instead of water-lilies floating plants such as duckweed or frog-bit are sometimes used. The shallow roots of these simply dangle in the water so that the actual depth of the pool does not matter. Usually the floating plants have small, and not very attractive flowers, but as well as using such plants for shade the fish often browse on their leaves.

There is also a wide range of plants that live completely under water, and it is for these that the steps have been made round the pool. Some plants, needing a greater water depth, may have to stand on the bottom of the pond.

Fish should not be put into the pool until it has had a chance to settle down and the plants to become well established. As always,

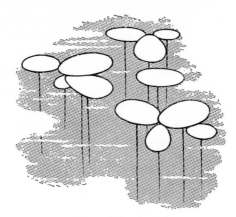

Fig. 26 Duckweed

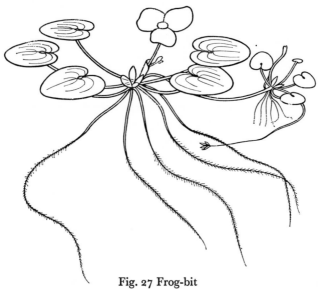

Fig. 27 Frog-bit

good young stock should be bought, and it should be introduced into the pond with care.

All varieties of goldfish will live together in a pool quite peaceably, but perhaps the hardiest species is the shubunkin.

Other coldwater breeds that may go into the pool without causing trouble include minnows, gudgeon, golden orfe, carp, rudd, green and golden tench, and the hi-goi carp.

Freshwater snails, pond mussels and newts are sometimes put into the pool, but they are not really necessary. Snails increase so quickly that they become a positive menace.

One creature that may move into the pool without waiting for an invitation is, of course, the frog, and the croaking of a number of these may be very annoying, particularly at night. There is little that can be done to prevent them getting into the pool, but it is possible to keep their numbers in check by cleaning out any frog spawn that may be found. This will be seen during the breeding season which lasts from May until July.

A certain amount of attention will have to be paid to the pool if the plants and fish are to remain at their best.

The feeding of the fish is slightly different from the system used for stock that is kept in an aquarium tank.

During the winter months pond fish are inactive and do not eat, and they may almost be regarded as hibernating. Feeding starts in the spring, but food is given only once a week. The feeding rate is gradually increased until mid-summer, when food is given twice every day. From thence onwards the rate tails off until no food is being given during the winter months.

In most winters there is a mild spell and during one of these the fish may be seen to be quite alert and reasonably active. This should not be taken as a sign that they are eager for food, and none should be given to them.

Apart from the differences caused by altering the number of meals and so on, the fish should be fed at the same time each day.

For pond fish a live diet is the most suitable. Earthworms are always appreciated, but if large they must be chopped up or shredded. To make certain of a regular supply of worms a piece of sacking may be laid on the ground in a shady part of the garden. If this sacking is kept moist by being sprinkled every night with water small worms will always be found on the underside of the sack.

Like their companions in indoor tanks, pond fish will always appreciate a change of diet. Scraped raw lean meat or liver, and crumbled yolk of hard boiled eggs are useful foods, and a certain amount of dry oatmeal may also be given. Micro-worms will be eaten with gusto, and most fish will take caterpillars, grubs and similar foods.

With luck, the number of goldfish and certain other breeds put into the pond will increase when the adult fish breed. Although a female fish may lay thousands of eggs a big increase in the number of fish cannot be expected. Life is far too dangerous both for the egg and the fry for many fish to grow to adulthood, unless either the existing adults or the eggs can be removed from the pool. The breeding of fish is considered in another chapter.

Because of the good conditions in the average pool plants usually thrive, but they need to be kept under control.

Occasionally the plants will have to be pruned by cutting out the excessive leaves. When pruning, the oldest leaves must be taken out so that the younger and more active growth is not strangled, and the leaves must be cut as close as possible to the main stem. Once a week (and even more if it should be necessary) all dead and dying leaves must be removed from the pool.

Plants increase in many different ways, and as the new growth comes along the older specimens can be removed. Plants that spread themselves by means of runners should have the latter cut through when the new plants have become firmly established. In the case of plants that have rhizomes (like the water-lilies) these will have to be lifted and divided in the spring. Catalogues from aquatic plant specialists will show the treatment needed by the different varieties.

A considerable number of different types of insect will attack aquatic plants, and various kinds of snail will do the same thing. The snails can be kept under control by pulling them off the leaves, but the insects can be much more of a problem. Insect-killing sprays can be bought, but if one of these is used it must be one that is guaranteed not to be harmful either to the fish or plant life, for some of the best known insect sprays can be poisonous to fish. Many kinds of insect pest are kept in check by the fish, who will feed off them, and the situation only gets serious when there are not enough fish to deal with the insects.

Algae, unless very thick, are no great disadvantage to a pool. If they get too thick a long-handled wire brush may be used to scrub them from the sides of the pool, but the algae cleaned off in this way must be taken out of the pond, and care taken not to remove any of the smaller fish with them.

Once a year the pool should be emptied. This gives a good chance to remove rubbish, mud and dead leaves, make any repairs that might be needed, and to scrub the inside of the pool. This sort of job should be done in the early spring, but before being started proper steps must be taken to ensure the safety of the fish. They will come to no harm if they are kept for a few hours in a bath or large bowl.

Even in the worst winter fish and plants should survive if looked after properly.

If it seems likely that ice will form during the night it is a good idea to float a rubber tyre on the pool. The elasticity of this takes a lot of the pressure away from the walls and may stop them from cracking. Once the water freezes any snow on the ice should be brushed off daily.

It is advisable to get oxygen to the water even during the most severe winter, which means that some small holes must be left in the ice.

This should **not** be done by knocking holes in the ice, particularly if it is thick, because this can set up shock waves that may harm the fish. If a small bottomless box is floated on the pool, and a few drops of oil are put inside it, this will often keep a small area free of ice. A rather better way is to stand a kettle full of boiling water on the ice. The heat will melt a fair sized hole and the kettle spout will stop it falling right into the pool.

After a thaw the water often looks badly discoloured, and this is usually a danger sign. The best thing to do is to empty out at least half the pool and refill it with fresh water.

In the summer the problems will be rather different.

The fish may be seen at the top of the pool, obviously trying to suck oxygen out of the air.

This is a signal that cannot be ignored. Squirting water into the pool from a garden syringe may be a quick, temporary cure, but it is also sound sense to change half of the water in the pool. If, after a short time, the fish are still showing signs of distress, something more drastic must be done. It may be that there are far too many fish in the pool, which means that some must be moved. On the other hand it may be that the water is poisonous because of decomposing dead fish, rotting food, and so on. The pond will then have to be cleaned out thoroughly and replanted.

Pond fish are easily trained to come to the side of the pool for feeding. As long as food is given at the same time each day, and from the same side of the pool, they will soon get the right idea.

Fish kept in outdoor pools have two natural enemies. These are birds and cats.

Not every species of bird will haunt a pool in search of a free meal, and the fish-keeper living in the town is often safe from such trouble. There is not a great deal that can be done to protect the fish. The depth of the pool may be a great help but in warm, sunny weather the fish will come up closer to the surface (and so into the danger zone) than they will on the cooler days.

The best way of defeating the cat is to take advantage of its hunting habits.

If a cat is watched while it is fishing it will be seen that it puts one paw into the water and hooks the fish out on to the grass to deal with it at leisure. There are a few cats who do not mind getting wet, but most of them hate the water. Ninety-nine cats out of one hundred would not dream of getting all four paws wet, even in the hopes of catching a fish.

Many fish-keepers therefore have a 'bog garden' on all sides of the pool. This is a narrow, shallow band of water, planted out with species that enjoy swamp conditions. The depth of water only needs to be 1 in. or so, and as long as the fish cannot get into this swamp they are safe.

8

Fish Breeding

Many fish-keepers, especially those with garden pools, have been surprised to find that the number of their stock has increased by the birth of young ones. In the pool these fish may not even be noticed for some time, because of their smallness and lack of colour.

This is proof that under good conditions goldfish and other cold-water species will breed and that some of the 'fry' (the name given to the baby fish) will survive.

Breeding that happens in this way is called 'uncontrolled breeding' because the fish-owner has not chosen the parents and planned for the breeding. It may be that the parents are not among the best of the stock held, and their young may be sickly and of poor shape. This is one of the reasons why fish-owners much prefer 'controlled breeding'. Not only is it possible to select the very best of the fish as parents, but it is easier to look after the eggs and fry so that some of the latter, at least, will survive.

It must be pointed out immediately that there is far more chance of success with the breeding of pond fish than with those kept in an indoor tank. However, it is possible to breed fish indoors.

All the coldwater breeds are egg-layers, and to get fertile eggs it is necessary to have a male and a female.

It is not easy to tell the sexes apart. One of the best ways is to examine the body shape in the spring, for the female's body will be much more rounded and plump than that of the male, because of the eggs she is carrying. The difference can usually be more easily seen if the fish are looked at from above in a shallow bowl.

Sometimes the male goldfish has tiny white pimples on the hard gill covers. If so, these marks will be very prominent when the fish is in good breeding condition, but not every male will show them.

In the natural state spawning takes place in the spring, but only if the fish are in good condition, well fed, and living in clean, well oxygenated water.

When spawning starts the male chases the female through the plants, choosing those that are in shallow water. The female releases a large number of eggs, but singly and at frequent intervals. The eggs are sticky and fasten themselves to anything suitable that may be handy, such as the plant leaves. As the female lays her eggs the male sprays them with a substance called 'milt' that he secretes in his body, and the eggs are fertilized by contact with the milt. Spawning may go on for several hours.

Once spawning is over the fish may start to eat the eggs and only those that are well hidden will escape. This is Nature's way of keeping the fish population under control, but in a small space like a pool or tank it adds to the fish-keeper's difficulties and partly explains why, in uncontrolled breeding, few fry are hatched.

In normal weather eggs hatch out in about four days but if the conditions are cold it may be as long as a fortnight before the young appear. When first hatched they hardly resemble fish, being tiny, thread-like creatures clinging to the plants or anything that will support and hide them.

Beneath the body of the fry is a small sac which is the source of their food during the first few days of life. If offered food during this time they will not take it, nor should it be given to them. When they have consumed the contents of the sac they become true, free swimming fish, ready to take proper food.

Fig. 28 Fry of fish with sac

More will be said later about the feeding of fry but we will now look at the differences in the controlled breeding of fish in a tank and those in an open pool.

It will be seen that if eggs are laid in a small tank they stand little chance of survival. For one thing there are likely to be more than two adult fish in the tank, and for another these fish have plenty of time between laying and hatching to find any eggs that they overlooked after spawning.

For controlled breeding a separate tank is needed and this should measure 24 in. by 12 in. by 12 in., though a shallower tank may be used if available. The tank should be set up a couple of weeks before it will be needed, one end being planted fairly thickly with aquatics and the bottom covered with a thick layer of coarse gravel. As this is not going to be a 'display' tank there is no need to plant it elaborately or do anything to make it look attractive. Rockwork is not needed.

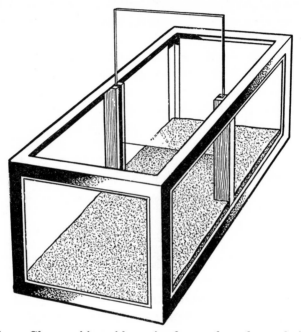

Fig. 29 Glass partition with a strip of grooved wood at each side

A piece of glass to divide the tank into two is wanted. If a slit is made down a length of rubber tube and a piece of this is put at each end of the glass the latter should fit tightly between the sides. A commercial aquarium separator may be used or home-made, grooved strips of wood will be adequate. The glass should be put into place at the time the tank is being set up.

The selected male and female fish are put into the tank, one in each half so that they can see each other but not come into contact. Healthy looking fish about twelve months old should be chosen.

The fish should be given a diet of live food such as daphnia and micro-worms. During this pre-breeding time no powdered food need be given, but the fish must be well fed without being allowed to overeat.

When the fish become really aware of each other they will spend long periods cruising up and down their side of the glass, keeping level with each other. After they have really become interested in each other the glass partition can be slid out. This should be done overnight.

Spawning usually takes place in the early hours of the morning. When it has obviously finished the two fish can be netted and returned to the main tank to join the other fish.

If it is intended to try to hatch all the fish (which might prove impossible) a number of tanks will have to be prepared well in advance. The plants (to which the eggs will be sticking) should be lifted, divided, and planted out into the separate tanks. Otherwise, the breeding tank can be left undisturbed.

When first laid, each egg is about the size of a pin-head. After a couple of days it will be easy to see which are infertile, as they will be of a dirty white colour and irregular in shape. Infertile eggs are a nuisance in the tank, and with care it is possible to lift most of them out on the end of a fine camel hair brush.

The hatching of the eggs has already been mentioned, and also the fact that the fry need no food until the egg sac has been absorbed.

From the time that the fry become true free swimming fish until they are about four weeks old is the period during which they are at their greediest, and need constant feeding. It is almost impossible to over-feed them at this time, though they cannot be given adult food.

'Infusoria' is the most suitable food for newly hatched fry, this being a form of tiny animal life that occurs naturally in ponds and streams.

It is not possible to rely on infusoria from natural sources and it is therefore bred.

Some water from an aquarium tank that has been in use for some months is put into a jam jar or similar container. Some fresh lettuce leaves are bruised and floated in the water and the jar put in a warm, dark cupboard. After about three days the water will be swarming with infusoria, each animal being much too tiny to be seen with the naked eye, though in the millions in which they exist in the jar they resemble a faint white cloud. A spoonful of this mixture is enough to make one meal for about fifty fry.

The only trouble is that after a few days the water develops a foul smell, and it is most annoying to have the jars in the house.

The best way to prevent this is to start jars at intervals of two days. This means that as soon as one jar develops a smell it can be emptied, and another jar will be ready to take its place. The first jar should be started the day after the eggs are laid if the weather is moderately warm, or the day after that if there is a cold spell.

Another way of breeding infusoria is to have a spare tank in the garden, this being filled with water siphoned from an aquarium that has been in use for some time. The lettuce leaves are bruised and floated in the water as before, and in a few days the tank will be swarming with infusoria. Whenever a jar of the liquid is taken out and fed to the fry, it is replaced with a jar of tap water.

This method of breeding infusoria has the advantage of keeping the container out of the house so that the smell is unnoticeable, but on the other hand the tank is exposed to insects and pests that could be a danger to the fry.

The simplest way of feeding infusoria is to pour a jar of liquid into the tank, or put a few spoonfuls into it, according to its size. Another way is to have a rubber tube between the infusoria jar and tank, so that the infusoria is siphoned out, controlling the flow by a spring clip to keep it at a steady drip.

Once the infusoria water starts to get foul it must no longer be used, as it may cause disease.

After two or three days on infusoria the diet can be varied with more solid food. This can be one of the dried powders but sieved so that only small particles suitable for the fry are given. It must be remembered that the fry have tiny gullets and they cannot tear their food down into small pieces.

Some of the firms making pet foods also sell food specially prepared for fry. These are really excellent, clean, easy to use and not expensive. They must be fed in accordance with the maker's instructions.

If healthy goldfish are to be reared they must be kept growing steadily.

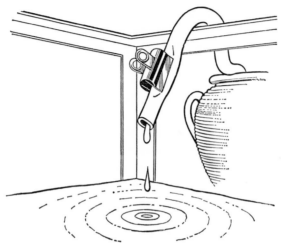

Fig. 30 Drip-feeding infusoria

When they are ten days old they need to be thinned out so as to reduce the number in the tank, and if there has been a big hatching several tanks must be ready so that the brood may be divided among them. Even at ten days the fry will be so small that they cannot be netted properly, so they will have to be scooped out of the tank with a cup or jug. If a really successful hatching has been achieved the hobbyist may have to get rid of three-quarters or more of the fry to give the others a fair chance of growing on into adults. It is wise to have a wide circle of fish-owning friends who might be happy to take some of the surplus fry.

The number of fry possible must be emphasized. The female may lay three thousand eggs and, with a great deal of good fortune, a thousand of these may hatch out. It may sound grand to say that you own a thousand goldfish, but you must have tanks in which they can be kept! So be prepared to dispose of fry before you have too many fish to cope with.

The size of the food given to the fry can be increased gradually until they are about one month old, at which age they should be taking adult fish food.

In spite of all the breeder can do fish will sometimes refuse to spawn. The only thing to do is to separate the fish again for another week or so, continue to feed them on live food, and then put them together again overnight. If this is not successful one of the partners should be changed. There is no need to be discouraged. Even experts cannot guarantee that fish will spawn, and the breeding of goldfish in a tank is never easy.

It is much easier to encourage spawning in a pool, though only rarely is a whole pool given over to one pair of fish.

To stand any chance of success the pool must have shallow areas in which the fish can spawn. It is possible to make artificial shallows by placing bricks, etc. round the edges of the pool or on top of the steps, covering these with pond gravel, see fig. 24. These shallows should be planted thickly but the centre of the pool should be free of aquatics.

Given five or six fish it is certain both sexes will be represented and it does not matter if the males outnumber the females, or vice versa. While this is not true 'controlled' breeding, it does mean that healthy fish can be chosen for the pool and, as pointed out previously, it is unlikely that the pool can be given over to one pair, with no guarantee that spawning will result.

Dried food is discontinued and the fish are fed on live diets, but, again, without being allowed to overeat. When a spawning is to be expected the plants are lifted, rinsed in a separate container to free them of pests and are replanted. Planting of aquatics in the shallows need not be done for permanency, so they can be anchored into place with lead collars.

Disturbances in the shallows warn that the fish are swarming.

In order to save the eggs or to limit their number, many fish-breeders lift some or all of the plants to which eggs are sticking and transfer them to a separate large tank that has been prepared in advance.

Fish that do not actually take part in swarming are likely to make an immediate attack on the eggs, and may be joined by the adults that spawned them. It cannot be too strongly pointed out that hatching after fertilization is automatic, and that the fish show no care for, or interest in, the eggs apart from their being a source of extra food.

Although it has been said that the egg-laden plants are transferred to a separate tank for hatching it is not advisable to use the ordinary glass-sided tank. In warm weather this may be far too hot during the early stages of hatching, and will harm the fry.

A shallow container, about 6 in. deep, is more suitable, and an old kitchen sink, plastic bowl, or something similar, can be very satisfactory. If it is necessary to use a glass tank the sides should be covered with layers of brown paper so that the light cannot strike through. The tank should be stood in a position where sunlight reaches the surface for a reasonable time each day.

The eggs will hatch out in the way described, and the treatment of the fry will be the same.

Some breeders pay more attention to the feeding of fry reared in an outdoor pool than to those bred indoors, believing that it is necessary to build up the fry more quickly. This is not so. Pond-bred fry will do quite well on the diets suggested above, but once they have passed the infusoria stage scraped raw liver and crumbled hard boiled egg may be fed with good results. In both cases the food must be reduced to such a fine condition that when put into the water it only tends to cloud it, with no large pieces of food floating about.

Goldfish are not the only coldwater varieties that will breed in captivity, and among the most interesting are the sticklebacks.

This breed is one of the few that build a true nest. The male does the building during the spring, making use of any suitable material (including plant leaves) that he finds in the pool or aquarium, cementing the pieces together by a sticky fluid that he secretes in his mouth. When finished, the nest is shaped like a small barrel and rests on the bottom of the pool.

The next thing he will do is to drive a female into the nest to lay her eggs, which he immediately fertilizes. His courtship is rough, for he prods the female with his sharp spines. When the female has laid her eggs she swims away and the male seeks out another mate with which to spawn. He repeats this with a number of females until satisfied with the number of eggs in the nest.

The male then mounts guard over the nest, both by day and night, fanning the water with his fins to keep it flowing over the eggs. During this period he is very aggressive, attacking any other male that comes near, or anything else (for instance a twig in the pond) that seems to threaten danger. The eggs take up to a month to hatch.

While the fry are small the male continues to guard them. If he thinks they should not be out of the nest he will take them in his mouth and put them back, and when they are a little older he will herd them back to the nest at any sign of danger. The female sticklebacks ignore both the eggs and the fry. The male obviously has a very busy time from the day he first starts to build the nest, and soon after the fry can look after themselves he usually dies of sheer exhaustion.

Another coldwater variety with an unusual method of breeding is the bitterling.

With this, the female lays her eggs inside a pond mussel, and there they hatch out. The fry swim outside the mussel but will quickly dive back inside it if any danger threatens. Although it is possible to breed the bitterling in an aquarium tank, success is more likely with pond fish. The pond mussel can only live and move about in a layer of mud, and it is more likely to find these conditions in a pond.

With all fish spring is the natural breeding season, so the fry are reared in relatively warm weather.

The colder the weather the longer it will take the eggs to hatch and the longer for the fry to become really independent.

Because of this, when breeding is done in a tank, some fish-keepers believe in keeping the temperature of the water at about 70°F, though this figure varies slightly according to the kind of fish being bred. The tank is kept warm by means of a small electric heater of the type used in a tropical fish tank; such heaters have automatic control so that the temperature is kept at a fixed figure.

This is a good idea if a large number of fish are being reared, but for the average hobbyist it is not really necessary to use heated tanks.

The breeding of fish is one of the most interesting branches of the hobby. It is also a branch about which there is a great deal to learn. Fish are living creatures with some sort of will of their own, so it often happens that in spite of ideal conditions and everything the owner can do to encourage them, the fish refuse to breed. Sometimes, in fact, a beginner will succeed in breeding fish under conditions in which an expert has failed. Luck plays an important part.

Those who would like to study fish-breeding in more detail should go along to the local library and study some of the excellent books that have been published on the subject.

9

Fish Ailments

In general coldwater fish are healthy and cause little trouble to their owners. Any illness that occurs is usually the owner's fault.

Nevertheless some illness may occur, even in the best kept tank, and the fish-keeper should know what to do about it, for in many cases a simple treatment will cure the fish.

Perhaps the most common fish ailment is digestive trouble.

This may be caused by overeating, contaminated food or incorrect diet. The sufferer is often one of the biggest fish in the tank, or a bully getting more food than he needs though goldfish do not, as a rule, tend to overeat. The fish suffering from tummy trouble looks out of sorts, is sluggish in its movements, and tends to drift around towards the bottom of the tank.

The cure is simple. Some water is taken from the tank, put into a shallow container, and the sick fish transferred to it. A few drops of medicinal paraffin are then sprinkled on top of the water. The fish will take these down without any trouble, and once it has done so it can be transferred to the main tank.

Fish should never be handled unless absolutely necessary, and when it cannot be avoided, a damp cloth or wet net should be used for restraining the fish once it is out of the tank. Fish must never be touched with dry fingers.

The reason for this is that the body of the fish is covered with a form of slimy coating, and if this is rubbed off tiny parasite spores can reach the unprotected body of the fish. This causes a fungus to develop on the body of the fish which, from its appearance, is sometimes called 'cotton wool fungus'. This fungus is contagious, spreads quickly from fish to fish, and may cause death.

It is not only handling fish that can start this disease, for it often results from an injury that breaks open part of the protective coating. This form of trouble is most likely to happen with fish kept in an outdoor pool. As a general rule a cotton wool fungus attack occurs at the end of the winter or in early spring when the fish are at their weakest.

Again, the cure is quite simple.

As soon as any fish is seen to have caught the disease an isolation tank is made ready, the water in this tank being of the same temperature as that of the main tank. One table-spoonful of salt is put into the isola-tion tank for every gallon of water

Fig. 31 'Cotton wool fungus' on fish

in it. The affected fish must be kept in the isolation tank until all signs of the fungus have disappeared, and if this tank is not needed for any other purpose the fish may spend another five to seven days of 'convalescence' in it.

The 'swim bladder' is an internal organ that helps the fish to con-trol its balance and course in the water. If the fish keeps to the upper part of the tank, cannot seem to steer itself (or even swim) properly, and particularly if it rolls about as it swims, trouble has developed in the swim bladder.

Certain digestive troubles may have much the same effect on the fish, but in that case it does not have a great deal of difficulty in movement but swims at an awkward angle. It prefers to keep to the bottom of the tank rather than the top.

For either complaint the cure is the same, the affected fish being moved to a separate, shallow tank. The temperature of the water in this tank is raised by a few degrees above normal, using a small electric heater of the kind used in a tropical tank. If the trouble is thought to be more likely an upset digestion than anything wrong with the swim bladder, the fish can be starved for a few days. In any case it may be better to starve the fish for a while, as no goldfish was ever seriously harmed by being put on short rations, even over a prolonged period.

After being kept for a few days in the slightly warmer water the cure should be complete.

Fish are sometimes affected by minute parasites; these include tiny flatworms called flukes, the fish louse (*Argulus*) and hydra, the latter being more dangerous to fry than to adult fish. Parasites are, perhaps, more common in ponds than in indoor tanks, but they can be introduced with live food or on aquatic plants. It has been said earlier that the fish-keeper should never rely on getting live food from local

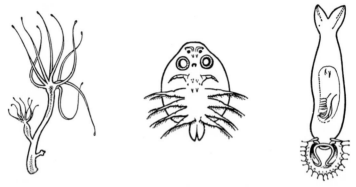

Fig. 32 Hydra (enlarged)   Fig. 33 *Argulus* (enlarged)   Fig. 34 Fluke

ponds but should buy it from a dealer who raises it under safe conditions, or breeds it himself. The washing of aquatic plants before setting them in a tank has also been suggested, and the problem of parasites shows how important these two simple precautions are.

When a fish is constantly scraping or rubbing against any convenient surface (such as a piece of rockwork) it is almost certainly suffering from parasite attack. The parasites will spread quickly from fish to fish and in a short time all the stock may be infected. Fish in which the attack occurs rapidly lose weight and the number of deaths may reach a high figure.

To clear the parasites the following treatment has been suggested.

Give the fish a special bath for three hours every alternate day until the condition is cured, the bath being given in a separate tank to which five drops of a 2% solution of mercurochrome have been added to every gallon of water.

When an outbreak of fungus or parasite disease has occurred it is a good idea to sterilize the tank, if a temporary home can be found for the fish.

The easiest way of doing this is to put crystals of permanganate of potash into the water until it is stained a deep shade of pink. There is no need to take the plants or gravel from the tank before sterilizing it. After a while the tank will take on its proper colour again, and it is then safe to return the fish to it.

Tail rot may occur in fish that have caught a chill and are being kept in overcrowded conditions. With this, the thin fin tissue connecting the spines starts to rot; the condition cannot be mistaken for fin damage caused by fighting. It is not a contagious disease but if it occurs with one fish in a tank the chances are that the conditions are bad enough for the other fish to be affected at a later date.

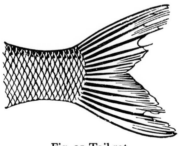

Fig. 35 Tail rot

The trouble is usually curable. The affected fish should be transferred to a less crowded tank, the water kept at an even temperature, and the fish should be put on a more suitable diet containing a high percentage of live food. After a few days the condition will start to clear up.

Sometimes the fish are to be seen at the top of the tank with their mouths above water as if trying to gulp air. This is not due to illness but if the fish are continually doing this it means that they are suffering from lack of oxygen. Almost certainly the trouble arises from overcrowding and can be cured by moving some of the fish to other quarters. Alternatively, the fish may have been forced up for oxygen because of poisonous gases in the water, caused by black sand or something similar.

It will have been noticed that for every kind of real illness mentioned above it has been suggested that the sufferer is transferred to an isolation tank. This does not need to be an elaborate affair, but if a sick fish is not put into isolation as soon as its condition is discovered it may be impossible to check the rapid spread of disease. Some kinds of illnesses are highly contagious, but in the early stages it would need a real expert to diagnose the trouble. The prompt removal from the main tank of any fish that is obviously in poor shape is one way of keeping ailments under control.

Bibliography

BOOKS

A considerable number of books have been published on all aspects of coldwater fish-keeping, and the following is only a brief selection of them. The list is made up of books that are readily obtainable, many of them being on sale in water-life stores. The publisher's name is given in brackets after the title of each book.

Anon *Aquarium and Pond Handbook* (Caperns Ltd., London)

Anon *Goldfish* (Ditchfield British Books Ltd., Leyland, Lancs.)

Anon *The Coldwater Aquarium* (Ditchfield British Books Ltd., Leyland, Lancs.)

Anon *Know Your Goldfish* (The Pet Library Ltd., New York)

Anon *Planting Your Aquarium* (The Pet Library Ltd., New York)

Anon *Garden Pool Construction* (Ditchfield British Books Ltd., Leyland, Lancs.)

Anon *Stocking the Garden Pool* (Ditchfield British Books Ltd., Leyland, Lancs.)

Betts, Leonard C. *The Goldfish* (Marshall Press, London)

Betts, Leonard C. *First Steps in Pond-keeping* (Marshall Press, London)

Brünner, Gerhard *Aquarium Plants* (Studio Vista, London)

De Wit *Aquarium Plants* (Blandford Press, London)

Evans, Anthony *Your Book of Aquaria* (Faber and Faber, London)

Evans, Anthony *Goldfish* (Muller, London)

Hervey, George F. and Hems, Jack *The Goldfish* (Faber and Faber, London)

Hervey, George F. and Hems, Jack *The Book of the Garden Pond* (Stanley Paul, London)

Latimer-Sayer, Derrick *Teach Yourself Indoor Aquaria* (English Universities Press, London)

Le Roi, David *The Aquarium* (Nicholas Vane, London)

Mannering, Rosslyn *Fishponds and Aquaria* (Cassell, London)
Perry, Frances *Water Gardening* (Country Life, London)
Perry, Frances *The Garden Pool* (Collingridge, London)
Vinden, John S. *The Pan Book of the Home Aquarium* (Pan Books, London)
Weigel, Wilfried *Planning and Decorating the Aquarium* (Studio Vista, London)

PERIODICALS

Two monthly periodicals devoted to fish-keeping are published in the United Kingdom, but it should be noted that these deal with tropical as well as coldwater fish.

The publications are:

Aquarist and Pondkeeper (The Butts, Half Acre, Brentford, Middlesex)
Petfish Monthly (254 Garratt Lane, London, S.W.17)
These can be obtained through any newsagent.

The *Aquarium Magazine*, a monthly American publication can be obtained through a few water-life dealers.

METRIC TABLES

These metric tables are provided to assist in converting the Imperial measurements used in this book

LENGTH

in	mm		in	cm
¼	6·350		18	45·7200
½	12·700		19	48·2600
¾	19·050		20	50·8000
in	**cm**		21	53·3400
1	2·5400		22	55·8800
2	5·0800		23	58·8800
3	7·6200		24	60·0599
4	10·1600		25	63·4999
5	12·7000		26	66·0399
6	15·2400		27	68·5799
7	17·7800		28	71·1199
8	20·3200		29	73·6599
9	22·8600		30	76·1999
10	25·4000		31	78·7399
11	27·9400		32	81·2799
12	30·4800		33	83·8199
13	33·0200		34	86·3599
14	35·5600		35	88·8999
15	38·1000		36	91·4399
16	40·6400		37	93·9799
17	43·1800		38	96·5199
			39	99·0599
			40	101·5999

AREA

square inches (in²) to square centimetres (cm²)

in²	cm²		in²	cm²
1·0	6·4516		16·0	103·2256
1·5	9·6774		16·5	106·4514
2·0	12·9032		17·0	109·6772
2·5	16·1290		17·5	112·9030
3·0	19·3548		18·0	116·1288
3·5	22·5806		18·5	119·3546
4·0	25·8064		19·0	122·5804
4·5	29·0322		19·5	125·8062
5·0	32·2580		20·0	129·0320
5·5	35·4838		21	135·4836
6·0	38·7096		22	141·9352
6·5	41·9354		23	148·3868
7·0	45·1612		24	154·8384
7·5	48·3870		25	161·2900
8·0	51·6128		26	167·7416
8·5	54·8386		27	174·1932
9·0	58·0644		28	180·6448
9·5	61·2902		29	187·0964
10·0	64·5160		30	193·5480
10·5	67·7418		31	199·9996
11·0	70·9676		32	206·4512
11·5	74·1934		33	212·9028
12·0	77·4192		34	219·3544
12·5	80·6450		35	225·8060
13·0	83·8708		36	232·2576
13·5	87·0966		37	238·7092
14·0	90·3224		38	245·1608
14·5	93·5482		39	251·6124
15·0	96·7740		40	25...
15·5	99·9998			

°F	°C	°F	°C
32	0·000	56	13·333
33	0·556	57	13·889
34	1·111	58	14·444
35	1·667	59	15·000
		60	15·556
36	2·222	61	16·111
37	2·778	62	16·667
38	3·333	63	17·222
39	3·889	64	17·778
40	4·444	65	18·333
41	5·000	66	18·889
42	5·556	67	19·444
43	6·111	68	20·000
44	6·667	69	20·556
45	7·222	70	21·111
46	7·778	71	21·667
47	8·333	72	22·222
48	8·889	73	22·778
49	9·444	74	23·333
50	10·000	75	23·889
51	10·556	76	24·444
52	11·111	77	25·000
53	11·667	78	25·556
54	12·222	79	26·111
55	12·778	80	26·667

VOLUME
cu. feet (cu. ft) to cu. metres (m^3)

cu. ft	m^3	cu. ft	m^3
0·1	0·00283	2	0·0566
0·2	0·00566	3	0·0850
0·3	0·00850	4	0·1133
0·4	0·01133	5	0·1416
0·5	0·01416	6	0·1699
0·6	0·01699	7	0·1982
0·7	0·01982	8	0·2265
0·8	0·02265	9	0·2549
0·9	0·02549	10	0·2832
1	0·0283	20	0·5663

CAPACITY
gallons (gal) to litres (l)

gal	l	gal	l
1/8	0·5682	7	31·8226
1/4	1·1365	8	36·3687
3/8	1·7047	9	40·9148
1/2	2·2730	10	45·4609
5/8	2·8412	11	50·0070
3/4	3·4095	12	54·5531
7/8	3·9777	13	59·0991
1	4·5461	14	63·6452
2	9·0922	15	68·1913
3	13·6383	16	72·7374
4	18·1844	17	77·2835
5	22·7304	18	81·8296
6	27·2765	19	86·3757
		20	90·9218

WEIGHT
pounds (lb) to kilograms (kg)

lb	kg	lb	kg
¼	0·1134	50	22·6796
½	0·2268	55	24·9476
¾	0·3402	60	27·2155
		65	29·4835
1	0·4536	70	31·7515
2	0·9072	75	34·0194
3	1·3608	80	36·2874
4	1·8144	85	38·5554
5	2·2680	90	40·8233
6	2·7216	95	43·0913
7	3·1751		
8	3·6287	100	45·3592
9	4·0823	110	49·8952
		120	54·4311
10	4·5359	130	58·9670
15	6·8039	140	63·5029
20	9·0718	150	68·0389
25	11·3398	160	72·5748
30	13·6078	170	77·1107
35	15·8757	180	81·6466
40	18·1437	190	86·1826
45	20·4117	200	90·7185